To Be Continued

REFLECTIONS on CHURCH PLANTING from ACTS 29

TO BE CONTINUED

THE UNSTOPPABLE MISSION OF JESUS

EDITED by TONY MERIDA,
CHRISTY BRITTON
& AMY TYSON

GCD Books

To Be Continued:
The Unstoppable Mission of Jesus

GCD Books
Austin, TX

GCD Books is a ministry of Gospel-Centered Discipleship. Our purpose is to produce resources that make, mature, and multiply disciples of Jesus.

To get more resources from Gospel-Centered Discipleship, visit us at GCDiscipleship.com/Books and follow us on Twitter @GCDiscipleship.

GCD editorial: Benjamin Vrbicek
Front cover design: Laura Schembre & Jeremy Writebol
Back cover & interior design: Benjamin Vrbicek

Paperback ISBN: 978-1-7367446-2-8
Ebook ISBN: 978-1-7367446-1-1

All emphases in Scripture quotations have been added by the author.

This book is dedicated to all the church planters tirelessly yet joyfully laboring to bring the good news of Christ's salvation for sinners to neighbors and nations for God's great glory over all the earth.

CONTENTS

INTRODUCTION

Tony Merida

The conclusion of a book or film always creates a reaction. The book of Acts is no different. It ends on a cliffhanger.

My wife, Kimberly, enjoys happy endings. When we watch a film that's sad or unresolved, I often say something like, "I liked that ending; that was very realistic." Kimberly usually responds with something like, "I don't want reality; I want a happy ending."

When the popular show *Lost* was nearing the last episode of the series, everyone wanted to know, "How will it end?" Many weren't satisfied with its strange ending, while others liked it. When I was a kid, I remember how a lot of my favorite thirty-minute shows would end with the dreaded phrase, "to be continued . . ." Today, many popular shows drag the viewer along for a whole season before giving some kind of closure.

What does the reader of Acts make of its ending? Luke takes the reader on a captivating journey, but the ending is a bit frustrating at first glance.

Up to Acts 28, Luke has led us to Paul's trial before Caesar, but nothing is said about that trial in the final verses. It's unresolved . . . we're left without answers about Paul's life. Can you imagine reading a novel and coming to this kind of ending? One may be tempted to write the publisher thinking that the book is missing a chapter!

But "to be continued . . ." is one of the main takeaways of the book of Acts.

All That Jesus Continues to Do

We must remember that Luke didn't intend to write a biography of Paul. He set out to describe the unstoppable progress of the gospel. His first book, the Gospel of Luke, described "all that Jesus began to do and teach, until the day he was taken up" (Acts 1:1–2a). The book of Acts, then, is about all that Jesus *continues* to do now that he has been taken up. That is, the story of Acts is about how the ministry of Jesus continued and is continuing, by the Spirit, through the church.

King Jesus is the hero of Acts, not Paul nor anyone else. Luke concludes Acts on a note of victory, with the king's triumph, as Paul exalts him in the mighty city of Rome. And this exaltation of Christ continues today.

So, Luke's message ends up being something like this: "This book is finished, but the mission isn't." Christians in every generation get to enter the story! My church and your church, and countless others are part of this ongoing, Christ-exalting mission. God replaces the messengers, but the message and the mission go on until the king returns.

Acts 29 churches recognize that we have the distinct privilege of continuing this mission. In the following pages you will read of how God's people are doing this around the globe. They are continuing this biblical, global, and Spirit-empowered mission.

A Biblical Mission

At the end of Acts, we read of the apostle Paul's relentless ministry of the Word. Luke tells us, "When they had appointed a day for him, they came to him at his lodging in greater numbers. From morning till evening, he expounded to them, testifying to the kingdom of God and trying to convince them about Jesus both from the Law of Moses and from the Prophets" (28:23). At the end of the chapter, we read how Paul taught all people about the king and the kingdom (28:30–31). From dawn until dusk, the war-torn apostle expounded Scripture, pointing people to Jesus.

From Paul's example, we're reminded of the necessity

of making disciples by teaching everyone about the king and the kingdom from all the Scriptures. Both the ending of Luke and the ending of Acts emphasize the primacy of Christ-centered exposition, first by highlighting Jesus's pattern of understanding and expounding Scripture (Luke 24:27; 44–47), and then with Paul's example.

It's such a joy to see brothers and sisters in Acts 29 be committed to exalting Jesus from all of Scripture—in large public gatherings, in classrooms, and in smaller, more personal settings. We recognize that Christians are not the only religion to have missionaries, teachers, and preachers. What makes us unique is *who* we commend, teach, and preach! We proclaim Christ from his Word (Col. 1:28).

As king, Jesus now reigns in the hearts of all who bow the knee to him. And he rules amid his enemies. Your local church has the blessing of serving as a little outpost of his kingdom. As the king's people, the church is called to display the values of the king and the kingdom, and to commend the king to the world. As we read and hear of many stories from the field, we see that Acts 29—this diverse community of healthy, multiplying churches—is doing these things by God's grace.

A Global Mission

In response to Paul's evangelistic exposition, Luke tells us that the Jews were "disagreeing among themselves" (28:25a), and they began to leave after he cites Isaiah 6:9–10. This was an appropriate text as it highlights how many are unresponsive to the gospel—in this case, the Roman Jews. This Isaiah 6 quotation appears in various places in the New Testament (cf., John 12:39–40; Rom. 11:8), always in contexts of unbelief and hardness of heart.

The Jewish prophets foretold this glorious salvation in Christ, and the evangelists preached it in the book of Acts. While many do reject this saving gospel, the book of Acts shows us that many people worldwide embrace it.

Initially, in the book of Acts, Gentile conversions were the exception, not the norm (e.g., Cornelius). But notice at the end of the book, Jewish converts are the exception, and Gentile converts (those among the nations) are the norm. In Acts 2:28, Paul turns again to the Gentiles (like he did in previous settings: Acts 13:46; 18:6).

God's kingdom encompasses the nations. Jewish evangelism must continue, but Christianity is for the globe because Jesus is not a tribal deity, but the Lord of the nations. As a diverse, global community of healthy, multiplying churches, we are seeing the gospel advance in all parts of the world, among all sorts of people, and for this we praise God.

A Spirit-Empowered Mission

The final two verses of Acts end this way:

> He lived there two whole years at his own expense, and welcomed all who came to him, proclaiming the kingdom of God and teaching about the Lord Jesus Christ with all boldness and without hindrance. (28:30–31)

Because the Romans weren't in a hurry to address Paul's situation, the apostle was able to receive all kinds of visitors. Though he couldn't go anywhere, he still was able to commend the gospel. Prison couldn't stop the gospel's progress, and we have learned that a global pandemic cannot stop it either!

Luke's final picture of Paul in the book of Acts is of his tireless ministry of the Word, proclaiming Jesus as king "with all boldness." Throughout the book of Acts, one cannot miss the emphasis on the Spirit-produced courage of Jesus's witnesses (cf., Acts 4:29–31). One of the signs of the Spirit at work in people is this holy boldness in evangelism and ministry.

The people in the book of Acts, including Paul, were clay pots. They were ordinary people. They were reliant upon the Spirit of God to continue the mission of God. Likewise, God has given *us* the necessary resources—the gospel and the Spirit of God. As you read the following pages, you will see how ordinary people of God, empowered by the Spirit of God, captivated by the Son of God, are accomplishing the mission of God, to the glory of God.

Without Hindrance

Luke concludes with an interesting phrase about the apostle's ministry of the Word, saying that Paul continued his bold teaching "without hindrance" (*akolutos,* 28:31). I think this is Luke's way of speaking about the boundless nature of the gospel. The message of the crucified and risen Christ triumphs over every worldly and spiritual barrier, regardless of what might come of its messengers.

Though Paul was chained up, the Word of God was running free (cf., 2 Tim. 2:9)! Luke has stopped along the way to highlight the spread of the gospel (Acts 6:7; Acts 9:31; 12:24; 16:5; 19:20). And this, the verse that ends the book of Acts, is the final reference to its unstoppable progress and the unstoppable mission of Jesus.

Today that mission goes on through faithful saints in large cities and small towns; through large churches and small churches; through those under oppressive governments and those in favorable settings; among various people groups and in multiple languages. In the following pages, you will read about the myriad ways in which Jesus is building his church, and insights that will inspire faithfulness to this mission.

This mission is "to be continued . . ." until Jesus concludes it, and we sing "Worthy is the Lamb" with people from "every tribe and language and people and nation" (Rev. 5:9, 12).

PART ONE | FOUNDATIONS

Foundation

: a basis (such as a tenet, principle, or axiom) upon which something stands or is supported

: a body or ground upon which something is built up or overlaid

– Merriam-Webster's Unabridged Dictionary

So then you are no longer strangers and aliens, but you are fellow citizens with the saints and members of the household of God, built on the foundation of the apostles and prophets, Christ Jesus himself being the cornerstone, in whom the whole structure, being joined together, grows into a holy temple in the Lord. In him you also are being built together into a dwelling place for God by the Spirit.

– Ephesians 2:19–22

These articles highlight the biblical foundations that compel, supply, and sustain our obedience. Motivation for church planting, the priority of the Word, prayer, community, theology in practice, the purpose of the church, suffering—these press together to form the ground upon which we stand, run, and grow. This section explores what the church is, why she exists, and why church planting is God's mission strategy in the world.

Jesus, who is himself our foundation, supplies what he commands and is the beginning and end of all our aims. In him, his church grows together into a holy dwelling place for the God who breathes life into dust.

1

THIS LITTLE CHURCH OF MINE, I'M GONNA LET IT SHINE

Christy Britton

Like many of you, I remember Sunday mornings gathered around a kid-sized table with other little ones. Dressed in our Sunday best, we ate cookies (the ones with the hole in the center you could stick your finger through) and drank Kool-Aid while our teacher led us in song. *This little light of mine, I'm gonna let it shine* . . . As our voices sang on, we declared (loudly and a bit off key) that we wouldn't hide our lights, wouldn't let Satan blow them out.

Now that I'm in my 40s, my cookie and Kool-Aid consumption has decreased, but some days I still hum the familiar childhood song. I appreciate its simplicity and biblical clarity, echoing Jesus's words:

> You are the light of the world. A city set on a hill cannot be hidden. Nor do people light a lamp and put it under a basket, but on a stand, and it gives light to all in the house. In the same way, let your light shine before others, so that they may see your good works and give glory to your Father who is in heaven (Matt. 5:14–16).

The world's darkness can be overwhelming. Our souls recognize the wrongness of fallen creation—broken homes, unwanted babies, sexual slavery, and more. But no matter how devastating the darkness becomes, there is One who has overcome it (John 1:5).

God is light (1 John 1:5) and has made us children of

light (1 Thess. 5:5). Essentially, then, a church is a gathering of light-bearers. We plant churches to create more communities of light. We plant churches that plant churches to reach the darkest corners of the world.

Consider three effects of a church that shines.

1. Darkness Is Exposed

Evil thrives in darkness. One of the great evils of our time is abortion. On December 31, 2019, as people all over the world celebrated the coming of the new year, Disrn News reported that the leading cause of death worldwide in 2019—by far—was abortion.[1] More than 42 million image-bearers were killed last year. To put this in perspective, approximately 6 million Jews were killed in the Holocaust.

Is your church devastated by the global slaughtering of unborn children? Then resolve to plant more churches. The horrors of this holocaust—and many other deeds of darkness—result from the sin of unbelief. "The way of the wicked is like deep darkness; they do not know over what they stumble" (Prov. 4:19). The only thing distinguishing us from the wicked is grace. God opened our eyes so we could turn from darkness to light and receive forgiveness for our sins (Acts 26:18).

As ones who've been delivered from the domain of darkness and transferred to the kingdom of Christ (Col. 1:13), we plant churches that expose sin by preaching the Scriptures. We invite rebels to repent and believe. Our bold proclamation—that Christ saves sinners—chases away darkness.

2. Goodness Is Visible

Our church plants must be communities of light that not only expose darkness but illuminate goodness. We were created in Christ Jesus for good works (Eph. 2:10), and his goodness is displayed when his people let their light shine.

---

[1] Adam Ford, "Abortion was leading cause of death worldwide in 2019 with 42 million killed," *Disrn News*, December 31, 2019: https://disrn.com/news/abortion-was-leading-cause-of-death-worldwide-in-2019-with-42-million-killed accessed Jan. 18, 2021.

When churches choose purity over pornography and care for victims of human trafficking, the world sees goodness against the backdrop of oppressive wickedness. When church plants include parents who treasure and train their children, and spouses who work through their differences to the praise of Jesus, our neighbors witness goodness.

The world's appetite for wickedness grows daily. So when our obedience to God's light-shining command likewise increases, we offer an alternative diet. Through our glad obedience, they can get a taste for something better. Something satisfying. With our good works we declare, "Oh, taste and see that the LORD is good!" (Ps. 34:8).

3. God Is Glorified

What do we want others to do when they see our good works? Give glory to God (Matt. 5:16). Our pro-life ethic isn't based on misplaced aspirations to fit within a certain tribe. We don't welcome the fatherless into our homes to create better Instagram stories. Our refusal to compromise our integrity to advance our careers isn't so we can play the martyr at small group. We don't shine for our sake, but for God's.

Our good works are fueled by the desire to see our Father in heaven praised. Our ambitions are aimed at his great glory magnified among neighbors and nations. We work heartily for him (Col. 3:23), and he is glorified through our actions.

I'm no longer the little girl who loved to sing about her light. I'm a woman who follows Jesus, the light of the world (John 8:12), and I'm gonna let my light shine. Yes, darkness abounds. But even the tiniest flickering dispels the dark. And we don't just flicker, we *shine* Christ's light into the dark and behold his mercy toward sinners.

Do you see the effect your church can have by letting your light shine brightly? And how church-planting churches can further spread the light? Let's courageously shine forth gospel grace, remembering that the darkness can never overcome the light (John 1:5).

2

HOW TO BE AN ANSWER TO JESUS'S PRAYER

Yancey Arrington

Have you ever wanted to be an answer to prayer? How about an answer to *Jesus's* prayer? Well, your church is.

John 17 is that prayer. It's the conclusion of what is known as the "farewell discourse," wherein Jesus informs his followers what will take place after his departure, tells them what they should expect from the world, and reveals rich truth about his relationship with his Father.

The discourse ends with Jesus interceding on behalf of his followers, akin to a high priest, and thus it has come to be known as the "high priestly prayer."

High Priestly Prayer

Contextually, Jesus's prayer appears to center on those who have believed in him up to this point in his ministry—his disciples (John 17:6). But he doesn't stop there. Jesus widens the circle and prays for the future witness of his disciples in the world:

> I do not ask for these only, but also for those who will believe in me through their word, that they may all be one, just as you, Father, are in me, and I in you, that they also may be in us, so that the world may believe that you have sent me. (John 17:20–21)

Jesus prays for the unity of his people through the ages. He's not just asking for any unity, but that which models the unity between the Son and the Father. It's a unity not only of spirit or mission, but of relationship. God means to display his glory in the church before the nations, so that the nations will come to glorify him in the church (see also Eph. 3:10).

The high priestly prayer is a hope-laden, faith-fueling prayer. Here we have the King of the universe interceding for his people. We aren't merely a *part* of God's plan for reconciling the world to himself; we are central to it. That's the glory of the church.

One with Christ

When Jesus expands the scope of his prayer to include "those who will believe in me through [the disciples'] word" (John 17:20), he not only reveals his heart for the future people of God, but also the *means* by which they will become his people.

Sure enough, as we read the book of Acts we see the Father answering the prayer of his Son. We see churches being planted, beginning in Jerusalem and extending to the ends of the earth (Acts 1:8).

Jesus's prayer, in other words, isn't just a prayer for the apostles; it's a prayer for church planting. Knowing this should spur churches today to consider partnering with like-minded church-planting organizations, be they networks or denomination-based.

When we link arms to plant churches, we continue to be an answer to the prayer of our great high priest.

Plant Churches

That's why my local church has prioritized church planting not just as something we do, but as who we are. It's why we've chosen to be part of a diverse, global community of healthy, multiplying churches in Acts 29. It's also why we founded the Houston Church Planting Network (HCPN). We wanted to see other gospel-centered, mission-minded churches demonstrate unity and reach our city. More than 100 local churches from various denominations have formed a coalition that has trained individuals from Asian, Hispanic, African American, and Anglo backgrounds and has planted approximately 50 new churches in the Houston area.

In addition to these new church plants, we've seen almost 100 future church planters enter into HCPN's training pipeline. We're seeing increasing numbers of churches joining HCPN, greater racial diversity among our planters, and a deep sense of unity through it all. This excitement is only surpassed by the thought that HCPN is one small way that the Father is answering his Son's prayer for the unity and expansion of the church.

So pastor, your church can be an answer not just to any prayer, but to one uttered by the Savior himself. You become an answer when you heed the call to church planting.

How will you heed that call? What groups can you partner with? Who in your church might have the potential to become a future church planter? Or is God calling you to plant? How can you foster a vision before your congregation for planting churches around your city, nation, and world? Whatever answers you find, remember that you're not just joining the mission of church planting. You're also an answer to prayer.

3

GIVE THE BIBLE FUNCTIONAL AUTHORITY IN YOUR NEW CHURCH

Reuben Hunter

For Dummies books have become a phenomenal success.[2]

Taking the complexities of anything from computer programming to French wine, and simplifying them for the everyman, sales have exploded. The reason for this success is doubtless because they tap into our desire to be given a simple way to master something that, otherwise, might take a long time. They offer a shortcut to success.

It's no surprise, then, that when it comes to church planting, there are plenty of "For Dummies" guides available. Christian publishers have missed the boat if they don't have their version of "Five Easy Steps to Successful Church Planting," complete with a foreword by their planter of choice.

On the whole, this is a good thing. We need all the help we can get. But the danger with many such resources is the underlying pragmatism and personal testimony that tend to win out over biblical teaching. Any church we want to see planted, if it is to be what God has designed it to be, must be established according to Scripture.

So, while there are many things that you *may* do as you plant a church, here's one thing you *must* do: give the Bible functional authority in every aspect of your ministry.

---

[2] This is an adapted excerpt from Reuben Hunter's chapter in *Multiplying Churches: Exploring God's Mission Strategy*, published by Christian Focus Publications.

Word-Centered Ministry

A simple glance at Paul's ministry reveals that proclaiming God's Word was given the utmost primacy. A brief overview of 1 Thessalonians 2 shows us this:

- "We had boldness in our God to declare to you the gospel of God." (2:2)
- "We have been approved by God to be entrusted with the gospel, so we speak, not to please man, but to please God who tests our hearts." (2:4)
- "We proclaimed to you the gospel of God." (2:9)
- "When you received the word of God, which you heard from us, you accepted it not as the word of men but as what it really is, the word of God, which is at work in you believers." (2:13)

Paul's ministry was—first and foremost—a ministry of God's Word. The reason for this is simple: God's presence and work in the world is mediated to us by his words. Throughout the Bible, from start to finish, his words create, sustain, give life, and sanctify.

This is why, when Paul passed the ministry baton to Timothy, he urged him to prioritize proclamation:

> I charge you in the presence of God and of Christ Jesus, who is to judge the living and the dead, and by his appearing and his kingdom: preach the word; be ready in season and out of season; reprove, rebuke, and exhort, with complete patience and teaching (2 Tim. 4:1–2).

And this is where we must start as we plant churches today.

Now, I realize this statement is not a great revelation to evangelicals. But that doesn't mean it's unimportant. We must remind ourselves of the priority of the Word in order that our practice on the ground reflects this reality. Without God's Word—regardless of what you're doing—your new church has nothing distinctive to offer your community. It offers nothing that any other organization could not provide to some degree. Indeed, without God's

Word, you will not actually have a church.

Therefore, we must never *assume* the centrality of God's Word. If we do, we will end up functionally prioritizing other things. These may be good and important things, but we err significantly if we allow anything to depose the Word of God from its central place.

So, to keep the Bible central in the churches we plant, we must cultivate discipline, humility, and faith.

1. Discipline

When you start—particularly if you're planting a church from scratch—if something is going to get done, chances are you'll have to do it. And there are hundreds of things you could do—fundraising, meeting people, developing a website, updating social media, formulating a Sunday-school curriculum, providing coffee and tea after the service, organizing your signage, advertising your presence, and so on.

These are all important. But on your priority list, they need to find their place underneath your careful study and preaching of the Scriptures. To prioritize God's Word like this—which involves saying "no" to good things—takes discipline.

2. Humility

When planting a church, many actions will get you a pat on the back, will make you look good. But few people will praise you for teaching the Bible week after week, for spending adequate time in the study. Building the church on God's Word is not glamorous, and it takes attention away from us. That is a good thing, but it does take humility.

3. Faith

The Lord Jesus Christ has promised that he will build his church, and we must receive that promise by faith. This is particularly the case in regions like Europe today, where the life-giving and sanctifying work of the Word is painstakingly slow. So, to keep God's Word at the heart of your ministry requires you to trust him.

Do you believe that the one thing your neighborhood and people need is the Word of God? It's really that straightforward. As Mike McKinley has put it:

> Teach God's Word. Evangelize using God's Word. Disciple people using God's Word. And then, when you launch a public service, preach God's Word.[3]

Keep Preaching

Finally, I want to urge you not to lose your nerve on the sermon. In a right desire to recover the importance of Word ministry in other contexts in church life, I think in recent times there has been a shift away from authoritative preaching. This is a mistake.

Paul instructed Timothy to "preach the word" (2 Tim. 4:2), and it's been the practice of the church down the ages. God's design is that his people gather to humbly listen to a man who stands in *his* place, to deliver *his* message—and through that event *his* Spirit works in power to bring *his* chosen purposes to pass.

May it be so in all our churches.

---

[3] Mike McKinley, *Church Planting is for Wimps: How God Uses Messed-Up People to Plant Ordinary Churches that Do Extraordinary Things* (9 Marks Imprint, Crossway, 2016), 53.

4

WHY I STOPPED READING THE BIBLE

Steve Robinson

"Don't depart from the Word."

That's the correct—and obvious—advice that all church planters, leaders, elders, and church-planting teams hear. No one in their right mind would contemplate trying to start and lead a church without being acutely aware of the importance of the Word of God. It must be central to every aspect of church life.

In fact, I've never met a gospel-centered church leader—or assessed a budding church planter—who didn't have the Word of God at the center of their plans for their church. Isn't that what the church is for? To showcase the wisdom and glory of God as we proclaim the gospel? To depart from the Word would be to drain the very lifeblood of the church.

And yet, there are many churches around the world for whom the Word of God is central, while they are led by people who leave the Word to the side in their daily lives.

How do I know this? Because I'm one of them.

Running on Empty

I love the Word of God. It's a wellspring of living water for my thirsty soul. But sadly, there have been many moments in my life when I've attempted to lead people to this living water while wandering in the Sahara myself. Even now—as I reflect on those times—I can hear the justification and excuses rattling around my head.

Finding myself in the proverbial Sahara was something that crept up on me. I didn't wake up one day and decide, *I'm going to stop reading God's Word on a consistent basis.* It happened slowly over time. Other things became more urgent, even more desirable.

We'd replanted a church, and it was growing. Another church had been planted from that church, and we had a third church plant in the pipeline. On top of that, our family was growing. God had given us a surprise fourth child, so we were in the process of moving to a new house. We were also recovering from an emergency treatment that our eldest daughter had to have (oh, and the dog died in the middle of all this tumult).

Little did I know, I was running on empty. I'm not talking about a lack of capacity to live in the midst of life's difficulties; I mean empty of *life*. As I slowly departed from the Word of God, I was closing the conduit through which living waters were to flow to me. I was in free fall, trying to lead a church to Jesus without spending enough time with him myself.

Restoration

My co-pastor stepped in and, in love, confronted me. He'd been trying to catch my attention for months, but I was avoiding him (which was awkward, given that we share an office).

When he asked me if I was consistently reading God's Word, I think he already knew the honest answer. I'll never forget what he said next: "Steve, you're looking for life in the midst of chaos, but you're avoiding the very place you know you need to go to find it." He was right. I'd been running from God and his Word—not because I didn't love him—but because I didn't want to face my sin.

But God's Word truly does heal and restore. My co-pastor and I spent weeks reading and praying through Psalm 119. By God's grace, gospel wind began to blow in my sails again. I was on my way out of the Sahara, being brought back to the fountain of life.

As I was refreshed and restored by the Word, I was reminded how desperately I need it. I need to be reminded, every day, of who God is and who I am in Christ.

I even preached through sections of Psalm 119. As I did so, I shared my struggles, confessed my sin, and sought forgiveness from the flock that I've been given the privilege of leading.

Church planter: do you want to know the most important thing you can do in your ministry? Chain yourself to the Word of God. I know you have a million and one things to do. I know the needs of your congregation feel unending. But if the Word isn't your lifeline, you won't have anything to offer your needy people.

Fountain of Life

My time in Psalm 119 was life-changing. Here are a few things the Lord taught me during this season:

When trouble and anguish find me out, God's Word is my delight (Ps. 119:143)

Trouble and strife will come your way, as they came to me. It's inevitable, and it comes with the territory of being a believer (never mind a church planter). Life's difficulties will expose what's going on in your heart. The Word of God was the ballast that kept the psalmist steady—and it could do the same for me—in the midst of many troubles.

God's Word gives me understanding, that I may live (Ps. 119:144)

The temptation to quit will cross your mind at some point, even if just for a moment. I wanted to run away, and the thought of pressing on scared me. I needed clarity, truth, and understanding. The Word of God gave me language to make sense of what was happening. More than anything else, the Word showed me Jesus (John 5:39). I was reminded of him who "for the joy that was set before him endured the cross" (Heb. 12:2). Because of Christ, the true Word, I can press on and have life to the full (John 10:10).

God's Word brings comfort and joy (Ps. 119:76–77)

We all long for comfort and joy, but we often pursue it

in places where it won't truly be found. For me, the temptation was to run from the Word, thinking it would bruise and batter rather than comfort and refresh. But you won't find true, lasting joy anywhere else. Psalm 119 is teaching me to cling to the promises of God's Word. Only as I've held on to them have I experienced the comfort and joy that I so desperately need.

So, church planter: don't depart from the Word of God. Drink deeply from it, *daily*. It's what you—and your people—need more than anything else.

5

WHY I LOOK FORWARD TO THE PASTORAL PRAYER AT CHURCH

Tony Merida

I love our kids at Imago Dei Church. Each week I hear from many of these little rascals after the service, or through my stroll through the childcare area (we have more than 130 kids younger than 4!). Last week I asked the 4-year-old girl beside me during our final song, "Do you like church?" She whispered back, "Not really, but I like the music." I appreciated her honesty!

Other kids bring me pictures regularly—usually of me preaching with a pronounced beard and big Bible. I always like those. Recently, a 6-year-old boy asked, "Pastor Tony, how do you pray those long prayers?" I replied, "Well, I love praying for our people." To my surprise, he said, "I love it when you do that."

I didn't pray the traditional "pastoral prayer" in the early days of our church plant. By pastoral prayer, I mean *an extended time of thanksgiving and intercession*. I prayed—sincerely—but it wasn't until the last three years that I began to make this a priority. Now I often say, "I look forward to the pastoral prayer more than the pastoral sermon."

My pastoral prayer includes the following: a prayer of thanksgiving followed by prayer for all ages and stages of people; for all kinds of physical and spiritual needs in our church; for the children in our church; for the fatherless and others in affliction; for our city; for our nation; for our church planters and missionaries; and for significant crises—locally and globally.

I've learned a lot from Charles Spurgeon's *The Pastor in Prayer*, a collection of his Sunday-morning prayers.[4] (It was Spurgeon's prayers, not his preaching, that most struck D. L. Moody on his first visit to the Metropolitan Tabernacle.)

We all have our own liturgies in our services, and you may or may not have a place for extended prayer for the flock. But I'd like to offer six reasons why it has meant a lot to me—and to our church—to include this element in our weekly worship service.

1. It expresses gratitude to God and our need for him

The pastoral prayer openly expresses our thanksgiving to God for his grace, and our absolute desperation for him to come and work in us that which is pleasing in his sight (Heb. 13:20–21).

We're not praying to put on a show, for we know Jesus rebukes phony prayer (Matt. 6:7). We're praying because we want to acknowledge his steadfast love, and confess that unless the Lord builds the house, those who build it labor in vain (Ps. 127).

2. It expresses love for God's people

The pastoral prayer is also a way for me to express care for God's people. It's been said, "He who loves me most, loves me in his prayers." Praying for everyone, especially groups of people often neglected or alone in the church (singles, elderly, widows, grievers) helps them feel loved.

3. It explains the purpose of the gathering

The pastoral prayer demonstrates that the Sunday service is not about entertaining or impressing people. Pray longer than what's standard in many churches and people will see that your primary goal is not to satisfy a customer, but to seek and exalt the Savior.

Hopefully, they'll sense that something is different about your assembly. Good. Don't give the impression

---

[4] C.H. Spurgeon, *The Pastor in Prayer* (Banner of Truth, 2nd Ed., 2004).

that prayer is of marginal importance or that it's something reserved for smooth transitions in the flow of worship. As Mark Dever pointedly says, "Devote so much time to prayer in church that nominal Christians will grow bored talking to the God they only pretend to know."[5]

4. It engages God's people and teaches them how to pray

The pastoral prayer is a great way to engage the flock, guiding them into prayer. I often say, "I'm going to pray now, but I want you to pray with me." I think the sweetest sound I hear on Sunday morning is people agreeing with me and one another in prayer.

Further, this prayer time models thanksgiving and intercession. Many of our folks did not grow up hearing a father, mother, or pastor praying for them regularly. Because one of the main ways we learn to pray is by hearing others pray, this corporate prayer may have a great effect on believers' ongoing discipleship.

5. It emphasizes your theology and mission

The pastoral prayer effectively reinforces your theology and mission. You show what you really believe by how you pray. So, teach and train people through careful, Bible-driven prayer. Express your missional vision through prayer as well.

6. It engages unbelievers

Finally, the pastoral prayer motivates unbelievers to consider deep questions of faith. Hearing your heartfelt prayer helps them realize you know they're present, and that the service isn't just about believers. You communicate your desire for them to experience God's grace, not just endure a service.

This extended prayer time has been a tremendous blessing to me and to our church, and I aim to keep doing it and hope to get better at it. As our little ones grow up, I

---

[5] Mark Dever, *The Four P's of a Faithful Pastorate*, sermon dated December, 5, 2012, *9Marks*: https://www.9marks.org/message/four-ps-faithful-pastorate/ accessed Jan. 18, 2021.

know they won't remember a lot of my sermon points, but I do hope they'll remember their pastor praying for them each week. And hopefully, they'll mature into bold intercessors who love God and love praying for his people.

6

WHY I LEFT THE NFL TO PLANT A CHURCH

Eddie Williams

It doesn't get much better than living the life of an NFL player. Catered meals, private travel, throngs of fans, social media prominence; it's the good life. You even get to play as yourself on the Madden video game, which just adds to the fact that millions are already watching you on TV every week. What more could a guy ask for?

Maybe this is why I became a church planter. It provided a life comparable to playing in the league. Basically the same thing, right? Wrong. Church planting and playing in the NFL are on opposite ends of the spectrum.

Desire to Plant

When I entered the NFL, I already knew I wanted to plant a church one day. I met Jesus in college while reading the King James Version of the Bible, which I'd been given by a stranger. About eight months later, I sensed God perhaps calling me to ministry. I wasn't ready to plant a church at 19 years old (despite what I thought at the time), so the best course of action was to continue through college and see where football would take me.

In college, I was honored to be selected first team all-conference, as well as team MVP. The hype began to buzz in the coaching and scouting world. Not many players come out of the University of Idaho, so when one does, the entire state tends to get excited.

Despite all the personal attention I received, our team

was horrendous. We finished 2–10 my senior year. To add insult to injury, our season ended in a huge loss, and I blew out my knee, which significantly hurt my chances of being drafted.

I didn't expect God to use one of the most disappointing seasons of my life to prepare me to plant a church 10 years later. With nothing to do but sit on the couch and read while I recovered, I devoured the Scriptures. I read the whole Bible on that couch, and my sense of calling began to solidify. I was gripped by the glory and majesty of God. More than ever, I knew that, at some point, I wanted to plant a church.

Confusion

Despite my injury, I was drafted by the Washington Redskins in the seventh round of the 2009 draft. It was a dream come true. I'd spent my entire life working for that moment. It was even a promise I made to my mother on her death bed. Yet somehow, as I flew to D.C. for training camp, I felt utter discontentment.

My time on the couch the previous 10 months had done something to me. Feasting on God's Word had shaped me. I felt completely torn. It sounds crazy that someone could get to the NFL and not be happy, but there I was.

On top of all this, I needed a few unexpected surgeries, which only compounded the uncertainty about my future in the NFL. One morning, I went for a walk to pray, asking God to give me insight about what to do. I was contemplating quitting football. But as I prayed, I realized I needed to embrace where God had placed me.

I also realized that my discontentment was not neutral; it was offensive to God. Discontentment in our circumstances is discontentment with God himself. So I settled in and gave myself to glorifying him in the league. My vocation as an NFL player was valuable to God and, if nothing else, was a platform to share the gospel.

Transition

My football career of five years ended after I had back

surgery while with the Cleveland Browns. Most players experience some sort of existential crisis once football is over. For many, football is all they've ever known. But I knew exactly what I desired to do.

In each city my wife and I moved to while I was in the league, we joined a church plant. When football finished, we kept doing the same. After serving in ministry in the Seattle area for nearly two years, we decided to move to Salt Lake City. We met a couple who was there to plant a church, so we jumped in.

We loved Salt Lake, and our family became comfortable there. I was working for the Fellowship of Christian Athletes and helping to plant a church. We owned a nice home, and my kids liked the city. The dream of planting a church slipped to the back burner; we assumed we'd plant one day, but not for a while.

From the Comfortable to the Unknown

But God determines where he places his people, and when (Acts 17:26). After three years in Salt Lake, the doors began to fly open to plant a church in my hometown of San Francisco. I met a guy at the Acts 29 US West conference who lived in the city and helped me think through logistics.

Everyone was supportive—including pastors, family, and mentors. The only thing stopping us was our comfort. We weren't expecting to experience such comfort and stability in Utah. It was a stark contrast to life in the NFL, which was marked by uncertainty and instability; I could be fired at any moment, and we'd have to up and move to a new city or state. It was stressful. In Salt Lake—for the first time in our marriage—my family was able to take a deep breath and put down roots.

So even though the opportunity to plant a church in San Francisco seemed to fall into our lap, it wasn't an easy decision. San Francisco is the most expensive city in America. *Is God really asking us to sell most of what we have for something that might not work?* We longed for clarity. *Would this work? Would it be worth it?*

But God doesn't promise perfect clarity. He promises

to be faithful. He was simply asking us, "Come and see" (John 1:39, 46). Despite our lack of perfect clarity, the call was so palpable that we felt we'd be telling God "no" if we didn't go. So, we went.

We moved back to San Francisco in March 2017 and launched a Bible study in our home in January 2018. Since then, we've had a front row seat to God's faithfulness. We officially started Bay City Church in September 2018.

As a young church family, we're learning that God is often going to ask us to jump before he hands us the parachute. He wants us to trust him. And because of God's perfect track record of showing up when I need him, I'm learning to trust him in my weakness as I lean on his strength and labor for his fame.

7

SUSIE SPURGEON'S GOSPEL INITIATIVE

Christy Britton

I'm ordinary. I serve in backgrounds, not in spotlights. My gifts and skills, though valuable, are small. So when I'm confronted with the depth of darkness around me, when I witness lack and loss in the world, I'm easily overwhelmed. What can I do about it? Perhaps you, too, are tempted to adopt a posture of helplessness, to throw out a "Maranatha!" and go about your day. After all, what can you do? I think we're asking the wrong question. It's not "what can I do?" but "what is *God* doing?" He has already accomplished redemption and given us a mission—along with the time, talents, and treasures to carry it out. What we need, though, is a little gospel initiative.

Here are three things gospel initiative accomplishes in light of Susannah "Susie" Spurgeon's example.

1. It Raises the Cause of Christ

While best known as wife to the beloved "Prince of Preachers," Susie served a leading role on a church-planting team. Her journey into church planting began with searching for something that couldn't be found. In his biography of Susie, Ray Rhodes Jr. tells how she visited Bexhill, a seaside town in England, and asked a local gentleman for the location of a Baptist church. He replied, "Don't know, mum, never 'eard of no such people as Baptises' ere."[6]

---

[6] Ray Rhodes Jr., *Susie: The Life and Legacy of Susanna Spurgeon, Wife of*

Susie Spurgeon was a 63-year-old widow with significant health issues when she became the first member of a church-planting team. Awareness of the lack of a gospel-centered church in Bexhill propelled her into action. She prayed for almost a year when she received a visit from two friends, pastor J. S. Hockey and his wife.

This former student of Spurgeon's Pastor's College was searching for a new ministry. Again, Susie prayed. As she prayed, she believed God wanted the Hockeys to go to Bexhill and "raise a cause there to his glory." She spoke with the Hockeys, who agreed to join her in planting a church. The Hockeys moved to Bexhill and assembled a team eager to join the work.

2. It Exerts Influence in the Church

Over the next few years, Susie's role in starting this church was undeniable. She cast the vision for a building secured without incurring any debt. She led the growing team to depend only on the Lord and his people for the church's needs. She gave generously to support the work.

Her confidence in Christ to establish a church in Bexhill inspired confidence in its members. She challenged them to "rally around the preacher as a gracious, praying, believing people." Susie used her matriarchal status to set the tone for the church. God blessed their work and the church plant thrived.

3. It Fills Voids with Jesus

Susie saw the lack of gospel presence in Bexhill. When confronted with this emptiness, she worked to fill the void with the risen Christ. After her death in 1903, a memorial tablet was added to the church building's wall. Part of that tablet reads, "Through Her Initiative Under God, This Church Was Founded and Largely by Her Liberality These Buildings Were Erected." Susie's earthly labors were complete, but the work in Bexhill goes on today through the church she helped plant.

When Susie couldn't find a church, she didn't say,

Charles H. Spurgeon (Moody Publishers, 2018), 203.

"That's a shame, but what can I do?" Susie prayed, networked, gave, and influenced. Susie exhibited gospel initiative. And it is our confidence in God's redeeming power, not in our abilities, that emboldens us to be people of gospel initiative.

Instead of withdrawing, what if we advanced? Instead of assuming someone more qualified will step up, what if we took those first steps? I want to be the kind of Christian who, like Susie, sees emptiness and strives to fill it with Jesus.

The truest theology and best intentions won't get the job done. We need gospel initiative. When we join our God in his kingdom-advancing work, we stand with a multitude of ordinary saints raising the cause of Jesus Christ.

8

SHOULD YOUR CHURCH "TRANSFORM" THE CITY?

Reuben Hunter

Christians believe in transformation. After all, we are transformed people.

Individually, when one is regenerated by the Holy Spirit, Paul says that "the old has passed away; behold the new has come" (2 Cor. 5:17). That's a radical transformation if there ever was one. But we're also transformed corporately: "We all, with unveiled face, beholding the glory of the Lord, are being transformed into the same image from one degree of glory to another" (2 Cor. 3:18).

And as the "earth is filled with the knowledge of the glory of the LORD as the waters cover the sea" (Hab. 2:14), the effect of these transformed lives on our local communities will have the salt-like effect Jesus expects them to have (cf., Matt. 5:16; 1 Pet. 2:9–12). It's every church planter's dream that they move into an area and grow a church that has a *transformative* effect on both the lives and also the culture in a given area.

But what does achieving that goal actually entail? Plenty of churches put "transforming the city/culture" in their vision. But I fear there's a lack of clarity both in terms of what that involves and also how it should be achieved, and such confusion can easily lead a new church plant off-course.

To provide some clarity, I think we need to start with the age-old question of the mission of the church. Should the church see "transforming the culture" as her mission? At the risk of sounding like the class pedant, it depends what we mean by "church" and what we mean by "transform."

What Do You Mean by 'Church'?

When it comes to the church and her calling in the world, there's an important distinction to draw between what Jonathan Leeman calls the church's "narrow mission" and its "broad mission." He argues that God "authorizes a church-as-organized-collective one way and a church-as-its-members another way."[7]

The church's "narrow" mission is to *make* disciples and citizens of Christ's kingdom, while her "broad" mission is to *be* disciples and citizens of his kingdom. This means the church functions in different ways depending on the context. When she is gathered under her leaders and Christ is especially present with his bride (Matt. 18:20), the church's mission is to preach God's Word, administer the sacraments of baptism and the Lord's Supper, and bind and loose on earth what is bound and loosed in heaven (i.e., meaningful membership and discipline).

When scattered in the world, the church's mission is to live out her distinctive calling as individual disciples, in whichever sphere of life the Lord has ordained. This distinction helps us know our role, because as Leeman points out: "When someone asks me, 'What is the mission of the church?' or 'Is caring for creation church work?' or 'Does the church's work center on words or both words and deeds?' . . . [or, I would add, "Is the church's mission to transform the community?"], I need to know whether the questioner means the church as corporate actor or the church as individual members."[8]

The "church as individual members" must seek to love their neighbor through the service of others, according to their responsibilities. But the "church as corporate actor"

---

[7] Jonathan Leeman, Christopher J. H. Wright, John R. Franke, Peter J. Leithart, *Four Views on the Church's Mission*, Counterpoints: Bible and Theology (Zondervan Academic, 2017), 40.

[8] Ibid., 42

is not bound in the same way. She might choose to allocate budget or hire staff to that end, but she isn't required to do so.

The life of William Wilberforce illustrates well how this distinction works in practice.[9] The transformative cultural effect of Wilberforce's life and ministry was significant, but his work to abolish the slave trade wasn't the work of the "church as corporate actor." It was the work of a Christian in public life who—through his love for God and neighbor—pursued his ministry all the while being dependent on and formed by the local church's narrower mission.

It's famously said that when Wilberforce asked John Newton whether he should become a minister, Newton encouraged him to pursue politics instead. This point could be illustrated in millions of examples throughout history, and it highlights the kind of transformation we should hope and pray for in our different spheres of responsibility or influence.

Stay in Your Lane

God has established three basic governments in the world. The first is the family, with responsibility for health, education, and welfare (Eph. 5–6). The second is the civil magistrate, with responsibility for justice (1 Pet. 2:14). The third is the church (as "corporate actor") with responsibility to minister God's grace and peace (Matt. 28:18–20). Each has an assigned role, and therefore each should "stay in their lane."

What I mean is, the family does not administer baptism or the Lord's Supper. The state does not opine on church discipline. And the church does not declare war. We want churches to be present at the heart of our communities, but they don't take responsibility for every aspect of community life. The church teaches how our individual work should be done—honestly, diligently, before the Lord—but it doesn't *do* that work itself.

When it comes to the church's role in "transforming"

---

[9] See Joe Carter's article, "Know Your Evangelicals: William Wilberforce," *The Gospel Coalition*, April 23, 2012: https://www.thegospelcoalition.org/article/know-your-evangelicals-william-wilberforce/ accessed Jan. 18, 2021.

community or culture, we should see that this happens in the weekly rhythms of the gathering and scattering of church members—coming together each Lord's Day to be transformed by participating in Word and sacrament, then scattering to labor faithfully and prayerfully in whatever sphere God has deployed them. As in the case of Wilberforce and others like him, the "church as corporate actor" is the engine of personal transformation that drives any culture-transforming efforts of the "church as scattered individuals."

Only God Transforms

This is the simple, sovereignly ordained rhythm of the Christian life. Thus the posture of the local church should be one of faithful patience.

This posture is incredibly hard in a culture of instant-everything—especially for the activist personalities you usually find in church planters. But God is the one who brings transformation, and we are the ones receiving—in his time, on his terms—a kingdom that cannot be shaken (Heb. 12:28).

9

WHY WE RESTARTED OUR CHURCH

Tyler St. Clair

I love my grandmother's food. The grandchild of freed slaves turned sharecroppers, she grew up in Tennessee learning to make the best, even though she often had little.

Slaves were given the food scraps, the undesirable, and what was left behind. This is what they had to make their meals. I'm amazed when I taste my grandmother's saltwater cornbread, dressing, and sweet potato pie, knowing these dishes have simple and minimal ingredients.

Like soul food, some of history's greatest strokes of genius, waves of innovation, and means of advancement came from those who lacked something.

The Problem

Years ago, I felt compelled by the Lord to plant a church in Northwest Detroit. I'd spent my whole life here, and my heart ached for the lost and socially disenfranchised of my community. After I came to know Christ, he opened my eyes to the gospel barrenness, generational brokenness, and hopeless apathy destroying my neighborhood. I knew that only the gospel could change these things, just as Jesus was changing me.

After reading the prescribed books and attending the requisite conferences, I only felt less clear on the task at hand. I wanted people to know and follow Jesus, but I felt conflicted as I was taught how to "attract people," "pull off a service," and "build systems." It seemed I was being taught how to build a church similar to a party bus, not a war tank. Further clouding my vision were the conditions in Detroit. While there's much I cherish about my city—rich culture, amazing history, strong and resilient people—we also face tremendous issues here. Immense poverty and crime, a deteriorated education system, government corruption, broken families with generational cycles of abuse and neglect—these are some of the things that make up the fabric of my city.

Planting a church in one of America's poorest and most crime-ridden cities presents a myriad of unique challenges and often leaves me with more questions than answers.

The Solution

Acts 2:42–47 proved to be the solution I desperately needed. After much time and frustration, I went back to the "church-planting drawing board." I sought to recapture the vision: to plant a gospel-centered church that reached the lost in Northwest Detroit. I remembered what I was cooking and simplified my recipe.

After much prayer, fasting, and wise counsel, my wife and I decided to uproot our church plant and regroup. We realized we had people, but not a church. We met together on a Sunday, but there was little discipleship and transformation. We had begun planting what we saw around us, not what we saw in Scripture.

We ditched unrealistic methods for the dependency of prayer. I prioritized preaching, discipleship, and pastoral ministry. The Spirit led us to take small steps of faith, like we see in Acts 2. It was a humbling and thrilling time.

Church planters are called to establish families of faith rooted in the gospel: families that have godly leadership, deep relationships, and intentional discipleship in order to reach the lost.

Die to Self

God helped me to realize something simple yet life-changing: this is not about me. Never. The planting pastor is called to cross-bearing sacrifice, not to "likes," "follows," platform, or prestige. Philippians 2:3 is Paul's mandate against self-absorption. It's a needed word for church planters: "Do nothing from selfish ambition or conceit, but in humility count others more significant than yourselves." Are others more significant to you than you?

Church planters need godly people to keep them accountable. Planting a church does not negate the need for accountability, repentance, and encouragement. Your soul needs to be shepherded, corrected, and cared for. Planter, you can't do this alone.

I realized I would have many roles and responsibilities as the lead planter. But none of my responsibilities was to overshadow my role as *pastor*. In the whirlwind of church planting, we must cling to our shepherd's rod.

Leading a church is a humbling activity. We are often forced to say "no." We must learn to pass the buck. We see this in Acts 6: the apostles appointed deacons to meet the physical needs of the widows, so they could focus on the spiritual needs—prayer and the Word. We must realize our limited capacity and "equip the *saints* for the work of ministry" (Eph. 4:12).

A shepherd is not a CEO. The shepherd's task is to feed the flock, pursue the wandering, correct the rebellious, and comfort the ailing and broken. Planting a church requires faithfulness in the seemingly mundane.

What It's All About

About two years ago, a friend at a crisis pregnancy center approached me about meeting with a young man who had a checkered criminal past and one foot still in the streets. But for some reason, he was willing to listen to me. After many meetings and many tears—and being embraced by our church family—he and his girlfriend surrendered to Christ. Our congregation wept tears of joy as I married them one Sunday after our gathering.

Our joy continues to overflow as we watch other stories like this unfold. This is what it's all about: the gospel breaking in and giving life to the dead. This is why we plant churches.

10

DON'T SIDELINE THE WOMEN IN YOUR CHURCH PLANT

Alyssa Poblete

It was a day I'd been anticipating since the dawn of our new church plant. After years of prayer and preparation, and months of building a team, we were finally starting to feel like we had a church family—a group of people we belonged to and who belonged to us. Today was the first day of community groups. My husband and some of the men on his team had been preparing for months.

"So, what's the plan for all the kids?" I asked my husband that morning. He looked at me a little surprised and said, "Oh, I hadn't really thought about that."

We had to laugh. We live in two totally different worlds sometimes. For me, I don't go anywhere without considering my children, because I spend all day with them. My husband, on the other hand, functions most of the day only needing to think about where he has to go and what he needs to accomplish.

Church planting has given us many opportunities to recognize how unquestionably different our experience is in the world, but it has also proven how much we need one another.

When we first began talking and praying about planting a church, the driving force behind our plans was that God had called us to make disciples. Church planting was a way we could heed that call. The decision was made together; we both serve, sacrifice, and invest in our local church in different ways, but to a similar degree and with a unified mission.

Man's World?

And yet, even though we're both devoted to local church ministry, we haven't always had the same experience. Church planting has often seemed like a "man's world." The resources provided, the training given, and the relationships that form tend to be tailored primarily to men.

Many of our congregations today seem to function as if the great mission of church planting and making disciples was assigned to only a faithful few. Women tend to be underrepresented, underutilized, and silent spectators among those groups.

But my husband and I share a similar conviction: women are not only *helpful* to a church plant, they are *essential* to Christ's call to go and make disciples. Disciple-making doesn't happen without women. Without women, the mission suffers.

After all, the Great Commission is for the priesthood of all believers—brothers and sisters alike. Apart from the role of pastor/elder, the Bible is clear: women are called to be active participants in every facet of the life of Christ's church. When women are underrepresented or underutilized, the church cannot bear God's image effectively, and our collective mission suffers.

In fact, the Bible assumes women are co-laborers. Paul says Euodia and Syntyche "labored side by side with [him] in the gospel" (Phil. 4:3). Rather than seeing male headship as a contradiction to women co-laboring in the gospel, Paul taught that these two things go hand in hand.

While many pastors would agree with this point, the church's practice doesn't always align with its theology. It's not enough for a pastor to notionally agree that women are *permitted* to participate in the church; they need to see women as *essential* to the mission of the church.

Church-planting pastors have a unique opportunity—as they use God-given authority to forge a new culture—to put an end to unhealthy distortions that have been pervasive within many churches for decades. And women participating in the church play a vital role in helping the pastors foster this type of culture.

Pursue Women's Participation

For the church planter this may feel like a lofty task. Resources are few, leaders are lacking, task lists are endless. While you may not yet have formal avenues for women's involvement, there are practical things you can be doing, even now, to form and shape your church in a way that affirms the value and dignity of your sisters. Here are three.

1. Invite women's voices to the discussion

Women were made to reflect God's character and nature in ways you, as a male, were not. Their contribution is vital. Consider how you are creating avenues for women to provide input. God has given you authority; use it to shepherd and lead those—especially the women—under your care.

2. Identify and invest in potential leaders

There are gifted women in your church who need intentional investment. Find those women and be intentional about equipping them for the work of ministry. Be an outspoken advocate for their growth. You will depend on them in the days ahead.

3. Integrate women into your discipleship vision

Women's discipleship should not exist on an island but as an extension of your pastoral leadership. Take this responsibility seriously. Stay informed on what the women of your church are reading, listening to, and being resourced with. Take the lead on creating healthy structures and avenues for women to invest and be invested in, and invite women into appropriate areas of leadership and participation in the life of the church.

Word to Women

The church-planting pastor cannot bear this weight alone. He needs the willing participation of the women of his church in order to help foster a culture that prioritizes this mission. Ladies, your pastor needs you. Here are three practical ways to serve.

1. Be available

Take the priesthood of all believers seriously. The mission to go and make disciples was given to you. Let your church planter know that you understand the gravity of the call, and be ready and willing to serve. Ask questions like, "How can I be most helpful?" and, "What are our greatest needs as a church?" Lend your voice to the discussion in humility and wield your God-given dignity with faithfulness and respect.

2. Be teachable

Your voice will not have much effect or value if it is not informed by the Word of God. Invest in knowing the Word. Pursue biblical literacy. The church suffers when women don't know and love the Word.

3. Be faithful

Keep God's divine priorities for your life in mind, and give your life to making disciples in whatever context you're in. Church planting is messy. Programs may not be in place to ensure formal avenues for participation. But you can always invest your life in making disciples.

We, as God's image-bearers, both male and female, are "a chosen race, a royal priesthood, a holy nation, a people for his own possession, that [we] may proclaim the excellencies of him who called [us] out of darkness into his marvelous light" (1 Pet. 2:9). This is a conversation not so much about empowering women, but about how the whole church can be faithful to the Great Commission.

Brothers and sisters, your joint participation and unique design is necessary to the mission of the church. We cannot have one without the other. So pastors, invite women in. Women, heed the call seriously. May our churches reflect God's image more clearly in the days ahead.

11

MY GREATEST NEED AS A COLLEGE STUDENT

Bennett Hansen

I graduated from a conservative Christian university three years ago. Since then, I've been perplexed—and deeply saddened—by how many of my fellow classmates have compromised on the truths of the gospel.

It turns out that the leaders in my church were right when they said to me and other students, "For us, success is not getting you to a point of sharing your faith every day, or leading great Bible studies, or being the most theologically sharp student. No. Success for us will be seeing you walking with Jesus 10, 20, and 30 years from now. That's what we want more than anything."

While I'm far from the 30-year mark, I'm walking with Jesus today. But the choices of many of my classmates trouble me deeply. Watching some of them walk away from the greatest treasure in all the world is heartbreaking.

But it troubles me for another, deeper reason. It troubles me because I know my own weakness. I sense my own capacity for sin.

As I've watched several friends compromise on core gospel truths, I've had to ask, *Why not me?* As an 18- and 19-year-old, what kept me? Why didn't I give in to the cultural onslaught, throw away my faith, and become like the world? And what continues to keep me now?

Answer: the local church.

Instrumental Influence

Don't misunderstand me: I believe *God* keeps his people (Phil. 1:6). I'm not suggesting that the institution of the church somehow replaces "he who began a good work in you." But the local church is the *context* in which God keeps his people faithful to the end. Lone-ranger Christianity isn't just dangerous Christianity; it's unbiblical Christianity.

Not only was the church a faith-preserving instrument in God's hand, it was also a launching pad into ministry. I'm involved in church planting today because of the influence of my college church.

It's worth mentioning that I was part of a student ministry in college. But it was a ministry of the church where I was a member; it functioned under the authority of the church's elders. So I knew involvement in the ministry *was* involvement in the church.

But here's the common thread that runs through the stories of many of my classmates: they never invested in a church.

Here are four reasons why every Christian—especially the college student—should prioritize active membership in a local church.

1. Long Endurance

Any and every campus ministry, no matter how great it is, has a shelf life. A student will have three, four, *maybe* five years in college, which means they can only be connected to a campus ministry for this period of time. The influence of even the greatest campus ministry in the world is contained to a few short years.

Not so with the local church. If we want to see students walking with Jesus long after they cross the graduation stage, our priority should be to connect them to the place with enduring influence.

Sadly, many campus ministries remain isolated from churches in their area. Little effort is made to connect students with churches. At my university, an outdated list of churches was pinned to a notice board no one ever looked at.

More than that, for incoming college freshmen, what's not to love about a campus ministry? They provide fun, exciting, student-centered events. And a weekly large group meeting is basically the same as a Sunday church gathering, right?

Of course, there are huge differences between a local church and a campus ministry. Among other things, only one has been instituted by God and guaranteed ultimate success (Matt. 16:18).

But do most 18-year-olds know this? I sure didn't. To an 18-year-old without a robust ecclesiology, the local church is likely to look rather unattractive when compared with many campus ministries. I wouldn't trust my 18-year-old self to choose wisely between the two.

2. Intergenerational Wisdom

One of the church's most profound effects on me as a student was its intergenerational nature. During some of the most formative years of my life, I was able to spend time with families being shaped by the gospel. I saw husbands loving their wives, dads leading their families, moms managing their homes, and kids being raised in the "fear and instruction of the Lord" (Eph. 6:4). I cannot overstate the significance of ordinary life lived alongside individuals and families who treasure Jesus.

On Sunday mornings after our church gathering, I would go and talk with Jim, an 83-year-old saint who'd been walking with Jesus for more than six decades. I'd ask him how his week had been, and I'd tell him about mine.

Could I have done that with a fellow student? Yes. Would we have had more to talk about? Probably. Would it have been more comfortable? Yes, most of the time.

But what a fellow student *couldn't* do was draw on the same wisdom, established through decades of walking with Christ, and apply it to my life. Jim could do that, and there were many "Jims" in my local church who faithfully encouraged me while I was a student.

3. Deliberate Discipleship

The local church is the primary context for discipleship. It's where saints are to be equipped, and the body of Christ built up (Eph. 4:12). It's where elders have been appointed to care for the flock of God (1 Tim. 3:1–7).

As a student, I was more likely to be followed up with by an elder than by a fellow student (even if I saw the student daily and the elder only once or twice a week). It's no surprise that an elder was more faithful in shepherding me than a fellow student was.

4. Meaningful Sending

The local church was also the primary means by which God called me to the nations. I now live and work in a city in Northern England, where I'm part of a church-planting team aiming to reach unreached people groups with the gospel.

Apart from my church in college, I absolutely would not be here. It was instrumental—in every sense of the word—in my being deployed to the nations. Not only was I trained and equipped *through* my church, I was sent *by* my church—under its authority and with its blessing.

If we want to see students walking with Jesus for as long as God gives them (both in college and beyond), we must guide students toward the local church *while they are students*. Assuming they will commit after college is not enough.

And at that point, it might be too late. May we not let it be so.

12

PRIORITIZE CHURCH, EVEN WHEN THERE'S NO CHILDCARE

Kirsten Black

Before planting The Town Church in Fort Collins, Colorado, we attended a church in North Dakota that offered childcare up to (not through) age 2. At the time, we had a 1-year-old son, and I was pregnant with our second child. As the months ticked closer to Ezra's second birthday, I had a sense of dread well up in me, wondering how I could parent a 2-year-old through a service while tending to a newborn.

While my husband, Vince, was somewhat available to help, Sunday was a work day for him, and I was often solo-parenting. As I looked around, I saw all these families with young children who seemed to sit like little angels through the service. I felt ill-equipped and less-than as I sat in the last row with my rambunctious toddler and prone-to-scream newborn.

I was embarrassed for having "that" kid who kept whisper-yelling through the service, loudly announced he'd pooped in his diaper, dropped his juice cup no fewer than 300 times, drove his matchbox car up front during the sermon, and did any other number of things I was sure would cost Vince his job, or at least cause the church to seriously wonder about our parenting chops. It was a humbling season.

If I'm being honest, it didn't feel worth it.

As we enter a season where churches are returning to

modified indoor services due to COVID-19, many church plants don't have the resources or the space to offer childcare that meets health and safety standards. The thought running through every young momma's mind is, *But what about childcare?*

I want to encourage everyone who's finding this transition challenging. Moms and dads, make the effort to gather with your church family for worship, even though it's a struggle with small children. It's worth it.

Corporate Worship When It's Inconvenient

For those of us who are used to childcare during worship services, the absence of it is a harsh reality. By the time the service is over, you're exhausted from trying to keep the kids' masks on their faces, to keep them in their seats and away from friends, and to keep the baby from crying.

After loading up your precious cargo in the family vehicle you think, *It would be a lot easier to just tune in online.* If you stay home, there's no more fear of distracting other church members, or fear of what people must be thinking of you as a parent based on your kids' behavior. No more hassle.

But if we only prioritize corporate worship when it's convenient, our children will learn to do the same. We're training our children in their own worship of God by the way we worship during this really difficult season. We have a unique opportunity to teach our children about the importance of corporate worship. Let's not waste it.

Corporate Worship in Every Season

One of the most helpful things an older woman told me as I began having kids was that everything is a season—whether good or bad—and that every stage with kids comes and goes. The difficulties of corporate worship without childcare are no different. It may feel unending, but it's only a season.

A day is coming (much faster than you realize) when you'll be able to sit in a church service, take notes, consider the words being preached, and fill your soul-cup as you enjoy worship without the distraction of kids crawling all over you. But in this season, it's okay to lower the bar and worship how you can. Commit to making much of Jesus in the less-than-ideal circumstances of this time.

Corporate Worship Because Jesus Is Worth It

Christ has defeated our great foe. He's secured our salvation through his life, death, and resurrection. We're welcomed by the Father as beloved children and given an eternal inheritance. It's our joy to gather and make a joyful noise, to which our little ones eagerly contribute. We come together to worship King Jesus like the great heavenly multitude that cries out, "Hallelujah! For the Lord our God the Almighty reigns!" (Rev. 19:6).

You know those well-behaved children I saw in North Dakota? They weren't always that way. I learned the reason they were able to sit through church services: their parents taught them. They came back week after week, and patiently and painstakingly trained their children.

Parents, it can be done. I learned with my five boys. It's hard. It's arduous. It's tedious. And yes, it's often distracting. But it can be done, and it's worth it.

Don't let the absence of the church nursery, and the added inconvenience of meeting during a pandemic, keep you from gathering safely with your church family to worship the Lord. Church services may not look and sound the way they used to, but that's okay. There's so much grace. Bring the little children. Raise them up to worship Jesus.

13

UPHOLDING THE DIGNITY OF SINGLENESS IN THE CHURCH

Matt Hodges

I recently preached a sermon on singleness and was shocked by the feedback I received. Several single brothers and sisters told me it was the first time they'd heard singleness addressed from the pulpit, at least in a way that wasn't telling them how to date or find a spouse. One sister said it was the first time she felt as if her presence wasn't just *welcomed* in a church, but *wanted.*

My heart sank a bit hearing that one. It made me realize how much I wish I had preached—and built into our ministry philosophy—the dignity of singleness from the earliest days of our church plant.

Too often in church culture, we're inclined to idolize marriage and downplay singleness. But those who enjoy and steward the gift of singleness remind us that Jesus is enough, and nothing else can truly satisfy. We need this reminder.

Church planters, here are three convictions regarding singleness we should teach and implement in our churches.

Singleness Is a Gift

Christians sometimes speak of singleness as a gift—but not always in the way the apostle Paul intended. He upholds singleness as a gift in the same sense marriage is a gift: "But each has his own gift from God, one of one kind and one of another" (1 Cor. 7:7). The two kinds of gifts he's referring to are marriage and singleness.

The gift of singleness is not a spiritual gift or a unique ability to bear the weight of the single life. It's a blessing given by God for his glory and the joy of the one to whom it's given. Does singleness carry unique challenges? Certainly, as does marriage.

If we even implicitly treat single brothers and sisters as if they're called to some unbearable task, we rob singleness of the dignity Paul explicitly gives it. After all, given the choice, Paul says he'd rather the church at Corinth have *more* single people (1 Cor. 7:7–8, 26–31). Like marriage, singleness is a gift given to believers to glorify God and edify others.

Marriage Isn't a Prerequisite for Participation

Upholding the dignity of singleness means more than just teaching it from the pulpit. It also means structuring our ministries so that marriage doesn't inadvertently become a prerequisite for participation.

It's good to teach that singleness is a divine gift, but we must take care not to betray that conviction by subtly requiring people to check the "married" box before being able to serve and lead church plants in a meaningful capacity.[10]

When we do this, we communicate that to get married is to "graduate" from singleness and therefore become better prepared to contribute to the work of Christ's church. Of course, some of the biggest contributions ever made to the church were from single people. This isn't surprising, since Paul is candid in reminding us that singles have more margin to devote to the Lord's work (1 Cor. 7:32–34).

From both a philosophical and also a pragmatic standpoint, even implicitly deeming marriage as a prerequisite for service in the church doesn't fit with the text. If Jesus and Paul would feel out of place in our churches—as if

---

[10] For more on this, see Ligon Duncan and Sam Storms, "Empowering Singles in the Church," *The Gospel Coalition Video*, March 15, 2019: https://www.thegospelcoalition.org/video/empowering-singles-in-church/ accessed Jan. 18, 2021.

they're on the outside looking in—it's probably time to rethink some things.

Marrieds and Singles Belong Together

As the local church pulls God's future kingdom into the present, it provides both us and also the watching world a foretaste of what's to come. And the church is at its most beautiful when it embraces the myriad gifts God gives us.

A healthy diversity of married and single church members serving alongside each other creates mutual flourishing and edification. As Sam Allberry observes, "If marriage shows us the shape of the gospel, singleness shows us its sufficiency."[11] Single people need married people to show the type of love Jesus offers. Married people need single people to show that his love is more than enough for true and lasting joy.

When we segment single and married people into silos—community and learning environments with only those who share the same marital status—we stunt our church's ability to display the depth and dynamics of the gospel. Single brothers and sisters can demonstrate the sufficiency of the gospel and the call of discipleship with their lives in a way few sermons can.

Scripture makes it abundantly and repeatedly clear that singleness should never hinder fruitful and flourishing participation. In fact, *without* the meaningful involvement of single brothers and sisters, our churches will suffer. So as we plant and pastor, we would do well to teach the dignity of singleness and its unique blessings—and then to structure our ministries and leadership in a way that shows we believe our words.

---

[11] Sam Allberry, *7 Myths About Singleness* (Crossway, 2019), 120.

14

BROKENNESS IS NOT A BARRIER

Dave Furman

For years my wife, Gloria, and I prayed for the opportunity to plant a church in the Middle East. We even had a map with a square drawn around the downtown area of what was (at the time) one of the fastest-growing cities in the world. A pastor in a nearby region told us there was a need for a gospel-centered church in the heart of the city; we were compelled to pray that the need be filled.

After years of preparation, the time finally came. On August 23, 2008, we landed with our toddler on a steamy summer night. We were ready to change the world for Jesus.

After only a month in Arabia, however, everything fell apart.

Unexpected Pain

One day I was driving around the parking lot of a local mall, and as I made a left turn I felt a painful sensation in both my elbows. Soon after, boil-like wounds developed on my fingertips, and I lost use of much of my arms. I was unable to write, open a door, shake a hand, or get dressed. This pain wasn't altogether new; I'd had surgery on both my arms before we moved overseas to relieve a nerve disorder.

But we thought I was healed. To see the painful disability return was a crushing blow.

And that was only the beginning of a dark season.

Soon, depression would unleash its fury on my soul. I quit language school and sat on the couch all day, every day. It felt like God brought me to the desert to destroy me. I dreamed about having healthy arms and played an endless "if only" game: *If only my arms were healthy, then I'd be happy.*

But good health never came. Instead, the refrain in my head became, *I wish I was dead, I wish I was dead.*

No Fairy-Tale Ending

Fast-forward 10 years. I wish I had a fairy-tale ending to share, but I'm still disabled. I'm unable to do normal, everyday things: play ball with my kids, drive our car, open the car door or put my seatbelt on by myself. I can't even pick up a glass of water or hold a book. I'm in pain 100 percent of the time. Joy is a daily, often hourly, fight.

I've tried a dozen procedures, four major surgeries, countless hours in therapy, a cocktail of medicines, and a variety of herbal remedies—all to no avail. I'm still weak and broken. My condition may remain until glory.

And yet, despite all of this, God is building his church. By his grace, Redeemer Church of Dubai was planted in February 2010—and people came. Several hundred, in fact, from dozens of nationalities.

We had an incredible partner church who sacrificially sent people and funding. We had bold evangelists who brought newcomers. We had a brilliant location in the heart of the city. We've seen countless people come to faith and get discipled.

Since our inception, God has enabled us to plant more churches around the country. We've been involved in church planting work in faraway lands, like the Philippines and Lebanon. We've started a theological training center and seen leaders trained and sent out.

Through it all, here's the most important lesson we've learned: *God* is the one building his church.

Weakness Is Always the Way

The apostle Paul knew what it was to be weak. He begged God no less than three times to remove a thorn from his flesh. But it remained. Perhaps Paul wondered what his ministry could have been—how much he could have achieved—had he not had that thorn.

But here's the reality: God didn't work in Paul's life *despite* the thorn but *through* it (2 Cor. 12:9). Weakness is part of God's plan. Moses led God's people out of mighty Egypt. David defeated the behemoth Goliath. Joshua and the Israelites defeated Canaan when their impenetrable walls crumbled. As J. I. Packer has said, weakness is always the way so that God always gets the glory.[12]

I once read about an ancient Japanese art form called Kintsugi. It's a fitting picture of how God uses us in ministry. Kintsugi, which literally means "golden patchwork," involves joining together broken pottery pieces with gold or another precious metal.

The artist takes the broken pieces of pottery—cups, bowls, or plates—and puts them together again to form the original items. Rather than hiding the flaws of the pottery, he or she highlights the cracks by sealing them with gold. The bowl's brokenness becomes its beauty.

Kintsugi is found in museums throughout Japan because the "broken" art is seen as more beautiful than an unbroken cup or bowl.

God's ways are not our ways. We naturally think he needs us to be strong. But his ways are more like Kintsugi. In his perfect plan, God has always picked broken people to do extraordinary things. He has planned to use pain for our good and his glory in ways we could never imagine.[13]

God Chose the Weak

I spent years as a seminary student, did several internships, and took part in a church-planting residency. I went to language- and cultural-acquisition trainings. Gloria and I raised funding, built a team, and were ready to go.

---

[12] J. I. Packer, *Weakness Is the Way: Life with Christ Our Strength* (Crossway, 2013).

[13] I first read about Kintsugi from a newsletter sent out by Community Arts Tokyo, which pointed out this very truth about weakness (January 2016). I have also written more about this in my book *Kiss the Wave: Embracing God in Your Trials* (Crossway, 2018).

And yet, God wanted to make it abundantly clear that *he* was building his church. I moved to the Middle East to change the world, but it soon became clear God was changing me. He was stripping my pride and redirecting my heart. God wanted it to be crystal clear to us—and those watching—that the spotlight would be on his Son. Church planting is about Christ's renown.

Weak and broken leaders, go plant churches. Hurting church planters, don't give up. The sick and suffering have often been turned down for ministry, but heaven's calculus is different. Since the Lord will use the weak (1 Cor. 1:27), let us press on, in our weakness, to plant healthy churches.

15

LESSONS IN RESILIENCE FROM AN AFRICAN CHURCH FATHER

Raphael Mnkandhla

As a young boy growing up in Zimbabwe, I never would have imagined I'd grow into a man who's a pastor in America. That boy couldn't have envisioned I'd be facing the challenges of leading a Pennsylvania church in 2020, wondering—along with many other planters and pastors—how to endure this season.

Constant fighting among believers, relentless criticism of pastors, and the many responsibilities added to our roles this year has been difficult. Every day I become more aware of brothers who have resigned, or who are suffering with physical and mental ailments.

Many church planters are asking, *Will my church last? Will I be able to endure?*

I've been steeped in the works of Athanasius, the fourth-century African bishop whose resiliency amid a life of controversy is an example to us all. Athanasius spent almost 50 years battling Arianism. As a result, he was exiled five times from his church, making him absent for more than a third of his term as bishop. While every exile surely felt like a ministry setback, he endured, leaving a legacy of faithfulness at every turn.

As a Ndebele man who has been told through our proverbs, "Ask for the way from those who have gone before you," it has been an honor to glean from Athanasius. Like my grandfather used to hold my hand as we walked, I've felt the firm hands of this church father who has become my companion on this journey.

I'm learning three lessons from Athanasius I believe are essential for church planters today: ministry resiliency is energized by valuing the Scriptures, disciple-making, and community.

Value the Scriptures

During his many banishments, Athanasius learned that though exiled from Alexandria, he was never exiled from God. He concentrated on the daily discipline of Scripture meditation.

Athanasius's deep reverence for Scripture can be observed in his early exegetical works, *On the Incarnation* and *Against the Gentiles*. As he battled heresy threatening the church, he didn't solely rely on his exegetical skills or wisdom to defeat his opponents, but on God's Word.

The Psalms found a special place in Athanasius's heart. He believed the Psalms were a wonderful diagnostic and pedagogical tool. He wrote, "They teach us to recognize the inner movements of our own souls, these words become like a mirror to the person singing them."[14] The Psalms were his prayer book through turbulent ministry.

This busy Bishop of Alexandria unwaveringly prioritized communion with God through the Scriptures, meditation, and prayer. Planters, may this also be our priority so that we may, like Paul, toil with God's strength (Col. 1:29). And if we think we can labor in other ways, may we hear Athanasius's advice that, apart from Christ, we can do nothing (John 15:5), but those who know their God will do mighty exploits (Dan. 11:32).

Value Disciple-Making

In his ever-turbulent ministry, Athanasius could've been absorbed in self-preservation, but he chose to engage in making disciples at the peak of Christian persecution. Athanasius would challenge us today the same way he did Marcellinus (a deacon in his church) when under threat:

---

[14] Robert C. Gregg (Translator), *Athanasius: The Life of Antony and the Letter to Marcellinus* (Paulist Press, 1980), 24.

"Do not desert your post as if you were forgotten by God, but call upon the Lord." Our post today remains the same—to make disciples.

We also learn from Athanasius how to make disciples in times of crisis. When exiled from his church and unable to preach, Athanasius effectively used the media of his day such that one biographer said, "He could valiantly do battle with his pen."[15] Every word he wrote was received by his followers with eagerness and by his opponents with trembling.

Even when Athanasius couldn't meet with his church, he found ways to communicate his message of hope and perseverance in Christ to his anxious people. Athanasius's example inspires us to remain vigilant in the mission to make disciples during tough times.

Value Community

History heralds Athanasius as a great leader, but critical to his story are the many believers who surrounded and supported him, especially the monks. He found a brotherhood not only deeply devoted to his fight for orthodoxy, but also sincerely attached to him personally. The monks demonstrated the power of community in suffering through neighborliness and hospitality, especially when many bishops abandoned Athanasius for fear of sharing his fate.

Athanasius was as great as the community that sustained him. He wasn't alone in the battle. He had people that kept going when he couldn't, and this strengthened him to endure in every trial. This is still true for us today.

As we struggle to not only survive, but to thrive in ministry in 2020, let us look, like Athanasius, to the perfect resilience of Christ. Let us be men and women who value God's Word, his commission to make disciples of all nations, and his desire for us to do this work in community with other believers. May Christ be glorified through what we value in challenging times, and may his church be resilient.

---

[15] Lynn Harold Hough, *Athanasius: The Hero* (Wentworth Press, 2019; originally published by Jennings and Graham, 1906), 96.

16

WILL EVERYTHING BE OK IN ITALY?

Jonathan Gilmore

Here in Italy, my neighbor's kids just left a gift for my wife and me outside our door. It's a drawing of a rainbow with the words *Tutto andrà bene!*: everything's going to be ok! This is a lovely sentiment, but Italy's casualties from the coronavirus have recently overtaken China's. Things don't feel even close to being ok in Italy.

As I write, hospitals are at breaking point or beyond—especially in northern Italian regions. Coffins are piling up, and many deceased are dying alone. Infections are high and show no signs of slowing. All Italy is on lockdown as soldiers are called on to ensure people respect the stringent measures. This is not merely an economic disaster; for some, their very survival is uncertain (migrants with no daily income, savings, or food). "Ok" isn't even recognizable in my country right now.

A few weeks ago, something distant suddenly came upon us unsuspecting Italians. Several factors make this pandemic harder for us. The coronavirus was initially minimized: "Oh, it's just the flu." Ours is the second oldest population in the world. The increasingly grave situation was compounded by panic travel from affected areas in the north to other parts of Italy.

Social distancing for most Italians is innately difficult as we contend with overcrowding of large families in small spaces, with no yards or gardens. Add to that the edginess and anxiety we feel as we hope nothing—including the internet—breaks down. Now, our normal way of life is gone. No going out, no getting together. In its place is growing unease and fear.

The psalmist was familiar with unease and fear, too. He spoke of a day of trouble in which his soul refused to be comforted (Ps. 77:2–4). As he moaned, his spirit fainted; he was so troubled he couldn't speak.

Fellow church planters, hear a little of my story and be encouraged and prepared in your own.

Church Plants in Italy

My church plant is part of the Acts 29 network. In Italy, we have 15 church plants, most of which are in the north. Some are in the most affected areas. For example, Francesco Arco is pastoring in Genova. His wife Claudia's father was hospitalized three days ago and has been placed on a respirator. He is alone. Meanwhile, the Arcos themselves have been unwell, and their condition is being carefully observed. Several church members are infected; a few have been hospitalized. Others have lost their income and must survive on rapidly dwindling resources.

This fellowship now meets online with their group almost daily for prayer and encouragement from Scripture. This is a vital lifeline. As their newer believers face this unprecedented challenge, they need prayerful encouragement and strong grounding in the gospel of Jesus Christ.

Serenissima Church, near Pordenone, planted by Rob Krause, is a multicultural, international church. Many within the church work in healthcare. Mothers go to work not knowing if they'll hug their children again. Neighbors live through the tragedy of sickness, separation, and death. Migrants with precarious economic stability live day-to-day with little material security.

Hope for Italy

And yet we see glimmers of hope in Italy. Just as the psalmist could, despite his anguish, worship the God who "works wonders" (Ps. 77:14), so we press forward knowing he is here with us in Italy, working wonders. A neighbor has begun to recognize his need to know God. A young couple preparing for marriage is growing in their faith and seeing that a strong marriage depends on more than financial security and friends to gather with.

A university student wants to know more about Christianity because he's unimpressed with the response both from empty, traditional religion and also from prosperity-gospel peddlers (strangely silent in these times!). Views and responders to online messages, devotionals, and interviews are growing. In this time of great need, many are rethinking their priorities and spiritual identities.

Pray for Italy

Please pray for Italy. Devastating statistics continue to be released. Hundreds are dying each day. This was unimaginable a week ago. In this growing tragedy, we cry out to our good Father. We weep even as we trust.

Will you pray for the gospel to be powerfully proclaimed and embodied by Italian Christians? Will you pray for church planters to lead their people through these days of distress, knowing that God hears (Ps. 77:1)? Pray for our churches to grow deep and strong. Pray that those looking on from the outside might see our hope and long to know our Savior.

Finally, church-planting pastors, prepare for what lies ahead. Stay focused. Keep the gospel at the center of everything. Exalt Jesus and make his name famous. *Andrà tutto bene*? Will everything be ok? We don't have to wonder; we know. Everything for us, in Christ, *is* ok.

17

YOUR CHURCH MAY NOT BE AS GOSPEL-CENTERED AS YOU THINK

Tony Merida

The book of Romans is about more than the "Romans Road." It's not just a book about individual salvation (though it certainly communicates this glorious message). It's also about gospel-centered *community* and gospel-centered *mission*.

Michael Bird says Paul is "gospelizing" the believers in Rome.[16] He wants every aspect of their lives to be shaped and empowered by the gospel. This is reflected especially in the latter half of the book. Therefore, Romans stands as a great book to consider, not only for theological clarity, but also for insights on gospel-centered leadership.

Before discussing the benefits of gospel-centrality, it's important to understand how it differs from other approaches:[17]

Gospel-Denying Churches: These shouldn't be called churches. Various cults and extreme brands of liberalism would fit this category. They deny the essential truths of the gospel.

---

[16] Tony Merida and Michael Bird, "'Gospelizing,' 'Gracism,' and Church Planting," *The Gospel Coalition / Acts 29 Podcast*, January 18, 2018: https://www.thegospelcoalition.org/podcasts/acts-29/gospelizing-gracism-church-planting/ accessed Jan. 18, 2021.

[17] The "other approaches" in this article are categories that originate from Femi Osunnuyi, who pastors an Acts 29 church in Lagos, Nigeria.

Gospel-Redefining Churches: Related to the previous category, these add to or subtract from the gospel. Examples include the prosperity gospel and the social gospel.

Gospel-Assuming Churches: These churches say they believe the gospel, but they rarely preach it plainly and deeply. It's "Christianity-lite." Leadership talks, therapeutic sermons, and practical-improvement messages fill the air.

Gospel-Affirming Churches: Like the previous group, these churches believe the gospel doctrinally, but the gospel is only meant for evangelism, and it is segmented out of the life of the church.

Gospel-Proclaiming Churches: These churches are known for preaching the gospel every week in corporate worship. But the gospel is still viewed as simply evangelistic. The gospel tips people into the kingdom, but it isn't taught as that which also shapes and empowers Christian living. Often what is communicated to believers is some form of post-conversion moralism.

Gospel-Centered Churches

These churches preach the gospel every week explicitly—but not just to the unbeliever. They also preach and apply the gospel to Christians, as Paul did for the Romans (Rom. 1:15). It shapes and empowers Christian ethics and the life of the Christian community.

For example, marriage is taught by looking at Christ's love for the church (Eph. 5:25); generosity is viewed through the lens of Christ's generosity (2 Cor. 8:9); the call to forgive is rooted in Christ's forgiveness of us (Col. 3:13); hospitality reflects the welcome of Christ (Rom. 15:7). Calls to social action—like caring for the orphan, the widow, the refugee, and the poor—are also made to believers with reference to their own identity in Christ.

Gospel Implications

We could give many reasons to pursue gospel centrality, but I'll limit it to five.

1. The gospel changes lives

If you are a church planter, pastor, missionary, or ministry leader of any kind, it's imperative that you have an unshakable confidence in the gospel. It is the power of God unto salvation (Rom. 1:16). God loves to *save* sinners, and he does so when the gospel is *proclaimed.* Further, God loves to *sanctify* his people, and he does this as the gospel is *applied.*

2. The gospel leads us to worship

The gospel transforms us from the inside out. And when affections change, everything changes. If a person loves Jesus deeply, it will change his or her behavior dramatically. Paul's theology regularly leads him to doxology (Rom. 8:31–39; 11:33–36).

3. The gospel lifts us from despair

Sin, suffering, and death cause us to despair. The gospel lifts the saints from dark nights of the soul by reminding us that God's verdict has already been pronounced; that though we suffer now, we're still in the grip of the Father's grace. Even death cannot separate us from the love of Christ (Rom. 8:31–39).

4. The gospel unites diverse believers in community

In Romans 8, Paul is exulting in glorious gospel promises. It's important to see the plural language Paul uses: "us," "we," "brothers/sisters," and so on. Paul is seeking to unite both Jews and Gentiles in Christ, so he labors over the beauty of the gospel for several chapters in Romans. He wants to help them pursue unity in the gospel, and to consider how they should love one another practically (Rom. 12–14). When we get to chapter 15, Paul's appeal to unity climaxes with this prayer: "May the God of endurance and encouragement grant you to live in such harmony with one another, in accord with Christ Jesus, that together you may with one voice glorify the God and Father of our Lord Jesus Christ" (Rom. 15:5–6). Paul is applying his theology to build a unified, diverse people.

5. The gospel fuels our mission

You can endure opposition when you have promises like those in Romans 8. When you have a gospel this big, you'll want to take it to the nations. Many don't have a passion for the nations precisely because they don't have a gospel worth preaching. So it's no surprise where Paul goes at the end of Romans. In chapter 15, you find that Romans is a missionary support letter. Paul wants to go to Spain with the gospel. Tom Schreiner says Paul could have been 60 years old at the time of writing! That's what a big vision of the gospel does: it fuels our global mission.

Pursue Gospel Centrality

So let's seek to create a gospel-centered culture in our churches and ministries. Exemplify gospel centrality in your personal life. Apply the gospel in your teaching. See the gospel in the church's ordinances. Pray the gospel. Sing the gospel. Saturate your groups and classes with the gospel. Advance the gospel through evangelism and church planting. Celebrate the gospel as lives are changed. Evaluate your ministry by carefully noting how the gospel is being proclaimed and magnified.

May we follow Charles Spurgeon's counsel:

> Keep to the gospel, then, more and more. Give the people Christ and nothing but Christ. Satiate them, even though some should say that you also nauseate them, with the gospel. . . . By the roadside, in the little room, in the theater—anywhere, everywhere, let us preach Christ. Write books if you like and do anything else within your power; but whatever else you cannot do, preach Christ.[18]

From the "roadside" to "the little room," in large worship centers to underground house churches, from cities to farmlands, from the urban poor to the suburban rich, from hard places to holiday places, let us keep what is of "first importance" (1 Cor. 15:3) *the main thing* in our lives, ministries, and churches.

---

[18] C. H. Spurgeon, *An All-Around Ministry: Addresses to Ministers and Students* (Ichthus Publications, 2014), 89.

PART TWO | CHARACTER

Character

: the attributes or features that make up and distinguish an individual

: the complex of mental and ethical traits marking and often individualizing a person, group, or nation

: moral excellence and firmness

– Merriam-Webster's Unabridged Dictionary

For an overseer, as God's steward, must be above reproach. He must not be arrogant or quick-tempered or a drunkard or violent or greedy for gain, but hospitable, a lover of good, self-controlled, upright, holy, and disciplined. He must hold firm to the trustworthy word as taught, so that he may be able to give instruction in sound doctrine and also to rebuke those who contradict it.

– Titus 1:6–9

What is distinct about a Christian attitude, lifestyle, and mindset? Particularly, what should distinguish a leader in Christ's church?

Charisma, physical appeal, strength, decisiveness, and boldness can sweep us off our feet, and introspection can look like wisdom. But do these things equal godly character? This section focuses on some of the attributes that must mark elders in Christ's church, and which grow increasingly vibrant in the lives of all believers delighting in Christ through the Holy Spirit's unstoppable, shaping work.

18

CHURCH PLANTERS ARE FARMERS, NOT ROCK STARS

Tony Merida

Farmers are anything but rock stars. They get up early and work. They sow, plow, toil, and protect. In all of it, they beg God for rain.

That's a good description of ministry. Ministry is glorious, but it's not glamorous. Like farming, most of our work goes unseen; it demands attention and endurance. And at the end of the day, we're desperate for God to give the growth (1 Cor. 3:7).

Often God does send rain, and those are rich and joyful seasons. Is there anything greater than seeing people come to faith, grow in holiness, and be equipped and deployed for ministry? Ministry is challenging, but by God's grace it also can be joyful and rewarding. Like elsewhere in our Christian experience, it carries both sorrow and joy, pain and pleasure, trial and triumph.

When we see fruit, though, we must never go around boasting about what "we did." (I've never seen a farmer "bragtweet" about the number of pumpkins he harvested.) No, our boast and joy must be in the Lord, who graciously uses us in his harvest field.

Farming in Christian Celebrity Culture

But sometimes we are tempted to want more, aren't we? In the United States, the pastor as celebrity is a real issue. Some people will only come to church if a particular pastor is preaching. Conferences are filled with speakers who draw a crowd. While not all famous preachers intend to perpetuate this culture, and conference designers often have good intentions, the fact remains that many aspiring pastors want to be just like these prominent figures. Imitating godly leaders is right and good, but often it's not godliness that compels aspiring leaders; it's the celebrity and fame they crave.

So what happens when new church planters, entrenched in celebrity culture, begin to evangelize in order to establish a new congregation—only to find it takes years to see results? Many give up. They fantasize about doing something else. Some take their eyes off Jesus and self-medicate, looking to porn or some other escape.

If fame is the goal instead of faithfulness, the planter is a walking disaster zone.

We have a need far greater than another 20 spectacular conference speakers. We need millions of faithful, Bible-teaching, gospel-proclaiming, people-loving farmers. And we need them all over the world—hard-working pastors who will consistently plant gospel seeds, keep their hand to the plow, and beg God to send rain.

Hard, Hope-Filled Work

Like farming, gospel ministry is often unseen, usually slow, and always exhausting. But it's worth it because the gospel is (2 Tim. 1:8; 2:8–9). Given our gospel mission, we *must* endure. And given our gospel hope, we *can* endure.

According to 2 Timothy 2, we can endure as we are strengthened "in the grace that is in Christ Jesus" (v. 1). Paul urges Timothy to live *on* the gospel—that is, on the enabling grace that flows from our union with Jesus. He doesn't say, "Be strengthened by your own power and resolve." That would be useless. Rather, he says, "Be strengthened by the grace that is in Christ." Only the grace of Jesus empowers all the exhortations that follow.

Paul then proceeds: "Remember Jesus Christ, risen from the dead, the offspring of David, as preached in my gospel" (v. 8). Think about that. Paul is saying, "Don't forget Jesus!"

It's easy to forget why we're farming. It's easy to grow weary when our gaze is locked on our circumstances. When your tank is empty, remember the tomb is empty. The empty tomb points upward to the occupied throne.

Ministry isn't glitzy and glamorous in the eyes of the world, but it's glorious in the eyes of God. One day, when we see Jesus Christ, the real Superstar, we will be glad we never stopped toiling, sowing, plowing, and praying.

19

WHAT CALVIN MIGHT SAY TO CHURCH PLANTERS TODAY

Dan Steel

Have you ever wondered what it would've been like to plant a church in 16th-century Geneva? Imagine starting a new church at the center of what's come to be known as the Protestant Reformation. At the very least, it would've been nice to talk with John Calvin (and others) about life and pastoral ministry. Even 500 years later, there's still much we can learn from Calvin and his compatriots that's applicable to our ministry today. This is why I'm thankful that a friend encouraged me to read Calvin's *Company of Pastors* at the end of 2018.[19]

Calvin's Legacy

Calvin's legacy is due—in large part—not simply to his writings, but also his gathering a "company" of other ministers around him. As he did this, he established institutions, practices, and structures that would positively affect people for centuries.

Calvin's *Company of Pastors* gives church planters a fascinating and insightful window into the practices of 16th-century Genevan church ministry. And as I've discovered, there's surprising contemporary relevance for us as we seek to faithfully plant healthy churches.

[19] Scott M. Manetsch, *Calvin's Company of Pastors: Pastoral Care and the Emerging Reformed Church, 1536–1609*, Oxford Studies in Historical Theology (Oxford University Press, 2013).

Church-planting pastors will find Calvin's work relevant in any ministry season. Here are four.

1. When we feel isolated

In modern-day Western culture, 'the self' rules. And this reality no doubt shapes our understanding and experience of the Christian life and, therefore, pastoral ministry. This—among other things—can cause church planters to feel isolated, frustrated, and burned out. In the worst cases, it can lead to leaving the ministry altogether.

As I read about Calvin's ministry, one thing that struck me is how he sought to actively foster a city-wide ministry mentality in Geneva. He consistently invested in the lives of other local pastors, often at great cost to himself and his ministry. For example, Calvin organized a weekly Friday-morning gathering where local pastors would listen to and critique an exegetical talk. They would then spend the remainder of the morning praying together and encouraging one another to press on in their respective ministries. It's evident Calvin understood the deep need for mutual encouragement and support in pastoral ministry.

So I've had to ask myself: *Am I more concerned with building my own ministry than I am about God being glorified through all the local churches in my city? Are there ways I could help to foster a generous city-wide vision in my context?*

I've tried to intentionally schedule time with other local pastors, get to know them, their churches, and actively look for ways to bless and encourage them.

2. When we're distracted by the latest ministerial "silver-bullet"

Central to all that took place in the Protestant Reformation was an unwavering commitment to the Word of God. This was evident in the expositional preaching, public prayers, and numerous writings. Additionally, Genevan pastors—under Calvin's influence—sought to visit every household under their care each year—with the aim of knowing their sheep well and privately opening up the Word with each of them.

So again, I've had to ask: *Is there a danger—especially for those of us involved in church planting—that we've lost our confidence in the power of God's Word? Do we too heavily rely on other (good) things such as leadership, personality, organizational skills, or even flashy websites and flyers?*

3. When we're feeling entitled and struggling with ministry hardship

Church planting, like any other Christian ministry, is not easy. But even a cursory read of Calvin's work reveals that pastoral life in Geneva was certainly no walk in the park. And in Calvin's *Company of Pastors*, readers will discover the messy truths of ministry life among a band of pastors who were fully integrated into the life of the city and countryside.

Personal struggles included substandard housing, a lack of finances, family and marital struggles, unpleasant and unkind church members, complicated church discipline issues, the reality of death and mortality (especially in childbirth), political strife, as well as persecution from unbelievers. In short, we can see that these brothers weren't ivory-tower theologians who simply wrote from a place of theory. They were battle-weary pastors and church planters who knew what it was to suffer as they followed Jesus.

This has forced me to ask: *In an entitled world that increasingly expects comfort, how can we better prepare ourselves for the reality of suffering as we follow in the footsteps of Christ? How can we grow in long-term personal resilience? How can we support and encourage each other to keep going past the initial three-year stint?*

4. When we're only putting out fires and not planning for the long-term

Our culture is increasingly frenetic and fast-paced. Of course, we know in theory that planting a church is more like a marathon than a sprint (though many of us are still sprinting!). One of the helpful challenges from Calvin's example is the importance of strategic forward-thinking. It's clear that Calvin sought to establish firm foundations that would enable and catalyze long-term gospel progress. For example, Calvin and his team set up a seminary and employed modern technology (in the form of publishing) that enabled pastors to be trained long after Calvin was gone.

So I've had to consider: *Do we have a long-term vision? Or are we too short-sighted and focused on the treadmill of week-by-week ministry that we can't take a step back and plan projects or structures to help enable growth and long-term fruit?* Partly as a result, I've reinstated a much-needed retreat day—wherein, once every six weeks, I get away to pray and consider longer-term plans and priorities.

When it comes to facing the challenges of today, may we listen to and learn from the saints who have gone before us.

20

CHURCH PLANTER, DON'T UNDERESTIMATE THE OVERLOOKED

David Doran, Jr.

I'll never forget the day the Holy Spirit smacked me across the head with a middle-aged woman.

Anna is a 32-year-old with a developmental disability. She came to faith a couple years into our church plant. Baptizing her was one of the clearest points of God's kindness in my ministry so far.

Anna is a wonderful, faithful member of our church—but she's not going to direct a ministry or lead a Bible study anytime soon. In fact, she struggles to read and comprehend the Bible for herself.

Anna doesn't fit many of the conventional programs of a church. She can't work in the nursery or children's ministry independently. Many of our Bible studies are at the edge of her capacity. This isn't because she's lazy or unmotivated about Christ's glory, nor is she distracted with lesser things. Rather, formal ministry positions are out of Anna's reach because of the wisdom of God. She's not built for those kinds of ministry.

But does that mean she can't minister? Quite the opposite—I've seen God delight in using the unspectacular in spectacular ways. But we, as pastors and church planters, must have eyes to see it. Here's what I mean.

Anna and Brenda

Brenda—another woman in our church—lost a loved one

recently, and it was hitting her hard. She was struggling. As happens far too often, most church members coming and going in life and ministry didn't notice the weight of their sister's grief. Amid their hustle and bustle to get the kids checked in, prepare worship materials, and keep their eyes peeled for visitors, they missed an important ministry opportunity.

But Anna, who'd only been a believer for a few months at this point, didn't miss it. She noticed Brenda's grief and moved toward her sister in Christ. Anna begun writing letters to Brenda. She called day after day to check in. Anna was lovingly relentless in showing Brenda that she was both loved and not alone in her grief.

Needed Rebuke

As I watched this relationship unfold, the Spirit used Anna's example to rebuke me in two ways. First, I was cut to the heart over my pride. I expected God to use *me*. After all, I'm gifted, trained, and experienced. I'm the *pastor*! But Anna—with great love and gentle humility—was teaching me things I didn't even know I needed to learn.

When God used Anna so beautifully, it surprised me. She didn't have any of the obvious gifts I'm prone to value above others. She wasn't "strategic." All of the sudden I realized the depth of my sinful self-confidence. I really thought that somehow my gifts and abilities were a necessary part of the equation. I'd nurtured the idea that I brought something to the table that God needed.

But in and through Anna, the strength of Christ beamed forth. In her weakness, his power was made perfect (2 Cor. 12:9). The Spirit was at work, and he wasn't waiting around for someone like me.

After I looked up from my prideful navel-gazing, I was enthralled with the beauty and power of the Spirit's work in the church. God was using Anna, even when her pastor and fellow church members didn't know how.

Humanly speaking, Anna is hard to equip. She doesn't fit our normal boxes for serving or leading. She's an easy disciple to expect little from, especially in church planting. But the Spirit is delighted to use her powerfully.

Surprised?

Should we really be surprised? "Now to each one a manifestation of the Spirit has been given for the common good" (1 Cor. 12:7). Praise God that he's not hamstrung by the weaknesses of men and women—the weaknesses of people like me.

Brothers and sisters, the Holy Spirit is the one doing ministry in your life and church. He delights to use God's people, even though he needs not one of us. If you've been tempted to take confidence in your gifts, training, or position, can I encourage you to repent and ask God for fresh dependence on the Spirit?

Ministering alongside brothers and sisters with mental and developmental disabilities has helped me to see what was true all along—the Holy Spirit is the only one who can heal the sick, mend the brokenhearted, and encourage the suffering saint. Don't ever forget that the Spirit is the only one who must show up for powerful ministry to happen. And don't be surprised when he uses the least spectacular saints in the most spectacular ways.

When you're just hoping your church plant will survive, it's easy to only seek out the polished, the put-together, those who will be an obvious "value add" to your plant. Beware of thinking that way. Beware of worldly calculus.

Amid all your visionary labors and busy days, don't overlook the "Annas." They are out there, and they are absolutely needed.

21

5 LIES SATAN TELLS CHURCH PLANTERS

Matt Hodges

Satan loves to lie. It's his chief M.O. in his efforts to thwart the advance of God's kingdom. And since the planting of churches is God's primary way of advancing his kingdom, Satan particularly loves to lie to church planters.

Some of his lies are obvious. As hard as it is to functionally believe at times, we at least *know* that our worth isn't found in our ministry output. We *know* that Christ's love for us and our identity in him don't depend on our effectiveness. But some lies—perhaps the most dangerous ones—sound more believable. Like the whispers to Eve in the Garden, they sound *just enough* like truth to be credible.

Over the past several years of planting, I've heard—and believed—some of these lies. Here are the top five.

1. If You Want Something Done Right, Do It Yourself

The balance between appropriate ownership of responsibilities and allowing others to carry the load is challenging. The captain must steer the ship. But he can't do that while manning the sails, checking for land, and reviewing the maps—at least not at the same time. And if he tries, he certainly won't do everything well.

You may have many gifts, and you might be more qualified, but there is likely someone else who can do that task better with their whole attention than you can with a fraction of yours. What's more, Paul tells us in Ephesians

4:11–12 that the role of the pastor is to equip *others* for the work of ministry. That becomes difficult if we insist on doing all the ministry ourselves.

2. You Must Do a Lot of Things to Be Successful

Ever wonder why Google won the search engine race against Yahoo, despite Yahoo once being in a position to acquire Google for only $1 million? It's because while Yahoo tried to do it all, Google focused exclusively on being a search engine. Yahoo's page consists of news, weather, tabloids, and more. Google's page is simply a search bar. And that's why today, you "Google" something instead of "Yahooing" it.

Planters are tempted to do it all. Social media floods us with pastoral FOMO as we're bombarded with ideas that create the urge to add a little extra to our ministry. Resist that urge. Say no to things, and say it often. Discover what you can do well, and do it. Be Google, not Yahoo.

3. You Must Be a Dynamic Communicator to Be an Effective Preacher

Few lies burden a church planter like the one that says faithful preaching can only look a certain way. We assume our churches will expect next Sunday's service to mimic what they share on Instagram and Twitter. Don't mishear me: preaching ought to be compelling and affection-stirring. Its goal is to elicit worship, not just disseminate information. As Tim Keller says, we aim to change the listener "on the spot."[20] But that can be achieved through myriad styles.

As pastors, we should strive to better our preaching. But we must remember that true power lies not in "lofty speech or wisdom," but in "demonstration of the Spirit and . . . the power of God" (1 Cor. 2:4–5).

4. Faithfulness to the Gospel Looks a Particular Way

It's a privilege to live in the information age. The amount of helpful content just a browser search or Amazon order

---

[20] Timothy Keller, *Preaching: Communicating Faith in an Age of Skepticism* (Penguin Books, 2016) 165.

away is a blessing. We can, more easily than ever before, learn from those wiser and more experienced than ourselves. But the downside of all this access is the lie that our ministry philosophies must reflect the most recent book we've read.

Effective church planting means knowing which variables are independent and which are dependent. While a church's tight grip on orthodoxy and commitment to its mission should never waver, the resources and contexts will change regularly. We must discern how to solidify the former and evolve with the latter.

Again, we learn from our brother Paul. He believed that matters of "first importance" remained just that: of first importance (1 Cor. 15:1–5). Yet he had no problem contextualizing his message and adjusting his approach depending on his circumstances (Acts 17:16–34; Rom. 14:14–15). Trying to implement the ministry philosophy of someone with a different skill set, or of a church with different resources is an exercise in foolishness, not faithfulness.

5. You Build the Church

All of these lies find their source in perhaps the most dangerous one that Satan wants church planters to believe: this is on you. If he can get you to believe that the church rests on your shoulders, he's succeeded in thwarting the advancement of God's kingdom, because now you're only building your kingdom. And he's more than ok with that.

Church planter, remember Jesus's promise: "And I tell you, you are Peter, and on this rock I will build my church, and the gates of hell shall not prevail against it" (Matt. 16:18). Jesus builds his church.

Satan loves to lie to church planters because we endeavor to bring about his greatest fear—the spread of God's kingdom on earth. We labor for what Satan loathes. We embrace what he tries to erase. So keep sharp. Stay alert. Our enemy stands ready to lure you with his lies. Remain faithful to your first love (Rev. 2:4) and trust the endgame to the One who is infinitely more capable than we are.

22

CHURCH PLANTING AND THE IDOL OF IMMEDIACY

Adam Ramsey

> *I think the besetting sin of pastors, maybe especially evangelical pastors, is impatience.*
>
> – Eugene Peterson[21]

I have a confession that both my wife and staff can validate. I like to move fast. I drive, read, think, decide, type, eat, and walk quickly. Woe to those who casually dawdle through airports or have the audacity to drive under the speed limit in the passing lane!

Too often my prayer has been, *Lord, give me patience NOW.*

Over the past few years, though, I've been learning to slow down. To be attentive to the Spirit's pace in our church. To be still before the Lord.

Idol of Immediacy

Generally speaking, church planters in first-world countries are about as patient as a 4-year-old on a cross-country road trip. *Are we there yet? How much longer?* comes the voice from the backseat of our heart.

I've pastored in megachurches of tens of thousands, in house churches of dozens, and sizes in between. In each season, my heart has been tempted by the allure of

[21] Interview by Mark Galli, "Spirituality for All the Wrong Reasons," *Christianity Today*, March 4, 2005.

immediacy. The idolatrous desire for instant gratification exists in every ministry context, but it can acutely haunt church planters as we navigate the tension of an abundance of vision and a scarcity of resources.

Church planters daily wake to a temptation to move at a pace at which the Spirit isn't moving. Looking through the window of our congregations, we notice a lack of congruence between what we desire for them and what we actually see.

The kind of leaders who burn themselves out, burn their marriages up, and burn their ministries to the ground are the impatient ones. Is it any wonder that Scripture's wisdom writings juxtapose patience with pride? For example, Ecclesiastes 7:8: "Better is the end of a thing than its beginning, and the patient in spirit is better than the proud in spirit."

Impatience is the pride of thinking our timing is better than God's.

Unhurried Ministry of Jesus

Like all runners lining up for their first big race, church planters must learn to counterbalance the adrenaline that propels us out of the starting blocks at lightning speed with a sustainable pace. Pastors, after all, are long-distance runners, not sprinters.

And yet, the unholy trinity that Jim Elliot dubbed "noise, hurry, and crowds" easily robs us of joy. There's certainly nothing wrong with a large and growing church. But shouldn't we be a little cautious of the very things Satan used to tempt Jesus on the front end of his public ministry?

First was the hurry of immediate gratification: "Turn these stones into bread" (Matt. 4:3). Second, the temptation to prove himself with a spectacular display: "If you're really the Son of God, prove it. Throw yourself off the temple and have the angels catch you" (Matt. 4:5–6, paraphrased). Finally, Satan baited his hook with global glory and power (Matt 4:8–9).

Each of these temptations—immediacy, legitimacy, and glory—have to do with timing. Eventually, Jesus's fasting would end, his identity as the Messiah would be vindicated, and the glory of earth's kingdoms would belong to him. But not yet. And in the "not yet," Jesus patiently trusts the Father's timing. Not once in the Gospels do we see him in a hurry. So why are we?[22]

Running at the Spirit's Pace

In his insightfully titled book, *The Patient Ferment of the Early Church*, Alan Kreider proposes that patience was one of the essential virtues of Christians living under Roman rule. Since God is patient, they determined that "they, trusting in God, should be patient—not controlling events, not anxious or in a hurry, and never using force to achieve their ends."[23] What wisdom for church planting! Slowing ministry pace in order to increase ministry longevity is a step *forward*, not backward, in fruitfulness.

The Western church doesn't need more leaders who mimic shooting stars, briefly streaking across the skyline of conferences and podcasts. Instead, we need farmers—those who understand the seasons and know what it means to wait.

Since God is in charge and more committed to his mission than we are, we can relax into the hardworking rhythms of sowing, watering, and reaping—while leaving the results to him. As James 5:7–8 reminds us:

> See how the farmer waits for the precious fruit of the earth, being patient about it, until it receives the early and the late rains. You also, be patient. Establish your hearts, for the coming of the Lord is at hand.

In a time of great haste, we must re-learn practices that lead toward patience. What if we not only pray outrageously big prayers for our churches, but also embrace godly limitations through a rule of life that leads to longevity?

---

[22] These two paragraphs, along with some other ideas in this chapter, are taken from my book *Truth on Fire* (The Good Book Company, 2021). Used with permission.

[23] Alan Kreider, *The Patient Ferment of the Early Church: The Improbably Rise of Christianity in the Roman Empire* (Baker Academic, 2016), 2.

What if we give as much attention to the kind of leadership habits that produce a faithful finish (for example, genuine plurality, honest friendships, regular Sabbath rest, and unhurried time in prayer) as we do to strategic plans for an explosive launch? What if we obsess more about our walk with Jesus than we do about our work for Jesus?

Patience grows when we remember that we don't need to see what's coming up around the bend—we just need to fix our eyes on him. The One who invented time is never behind schedule. And in that glorious truth is the power to face anything. Even waiting.

23

WHY HOSPITALITY IS VITAL TO CHURCH PLANTING

Tony Merida

Hospitality is so important that Paul lists it as a qualification for pastoral leadership (1 Tim. 3:2; Titus 1:8). But it is still neglected. Some pastors are so diligent to "not bring ministry home with them" that they avoid practicing hospitality altogether.

Gospel-centered leaders should set the example of hospitality. By opening up our hearts and homes to others in hospitality, we experience fellowship within the Christian community (Rom. 12:13; 1 Pet. 4:9), and we can do mercy ministry and evangelism toward those outside the Christian community (Luke 14:12).

I often tell prospective church planters, "In many ways, church planting is about learning to practice hospitality well. It's about meeting, welcoming, listening to, and loving people."

A church planter in Detroit told me about efforts to build "visible currency" in the early days of planting a church. He simply grilled hotdogs outside his house every Friday night during the summer. He worked hard to develop relationships in a hard place, and one of his main forms of outreach has been hospitality.

Another friend planting in a poor part of Raleigh put up a basketball hoop outside his house and stocked his refrigerator with popsicles. It's not uncommon for him have eight to ten boys from around the neighborhood at his house playing ball, drinking lemonade, or sitting on his couch watching football on a Sunday. His hospitality has opened many other doors for outreach in the area.

Gospel Motivation

Good hospitality is an outworking of the gospel. In the gospel, God is *hospitable* to us. In the beginning of the Bible, we find God caring for Adam and Eve in the garden.

As we trace the biblical narrative, we see God caring for his people in the wilderness. God's people are to welcome the stranger, just as he welcomed them (Lev. 19:34). God sustains his people until he brings them to the "land flowing with milk and honey." God welcomes, hosts, cares, provides, and blesses.

We see hospitality in the ministry of Jesus. He prioritized eating with people. Robert Karris says, "In Luke's Gospel, Jesus is either going to a meal, at a meal, or coming from a meal."[24] Jesus gets labeled "as a drunkard and a glutton, a friend of tax collectors and sinners" (Luke 7:34). He hangs out with people hated by society, like Levi and Zacchaeus (Luke 5:27–32; 19:1–10). After his resurrection, Jesus breaks bread with his disciples (Luke 24:30). And now, we remember his sacrifice and look forward to his return by way of a meal (Matt. 26:26–29; Mark 14:22–25; 1 Cor. 11:23–26).

The early church exhibited hospitality in numerous ways, expressed throughout the book of Acts and across the New Testament. The Bible ends with a glorious vision of the great wedding banquet (Rev. 19:7), and with God dwelling with his people (Rev. 22). There's an invitation for the thirsty to come to God and be satisfied forever (Rev. 22:17). What a gracious, hospitable God!

6 Ways to Grow in Gospel-Fueled Hospitality

To practice hospitality well, we need to lay down our idols and consider our context.

---

[24] Robert J. Karris, *Eating Your Way Through Luke's Gospel* (Liturgical Press, 2006) 97.

1. Expand your guest list

Jesus rocked people's world when he said:

> When you give a dinner or a banquet, do not invite your friends or your brothers or your relatives or rich neighbors, lest they also invite you in return and you be repaid. But when you give a feast, invite the poor, the crippled, the lame, the blind, and you will be blessed, because they cannot repay you. For you will be repaid at the resurrection of the just. (Luke14:12–14)

Jesus had already rebuked *the guests* of the party (Luke 14:7–11); then he corrected *the host.* When you have a party—Christmas party, birthday party, or some other significant event—invite those who *can't repay you.* Invite the marginalized. And you will be repaid "at the resurrection of the just." Jesus fills up ordinary events with eternal significance.

2. Serve others rather than trying to impress them

Many confuse hospitality with "entertaining." Entertaining is often about the host, not the guests. It's about showing off, not serving. You can be thoughtful without being extravagant. You don't have to wow people with expensive china and food. Aim for *warm* rather than *wow.*

Your goal isn't to draw attention to yourself, but to Christ.

3. Reject the "my home is my refuge" mentality

Jesus is your refuge. Anything else we make our "refuge" is idolatry. When it comes to our homes, we should think *stewardship* rather than *ownership.* A home is a place to welcome and love the broken. Hosting reflects the values of God's kingdom, giving people a foretaste of what's to come.

If you have a small house, consider other ways to welcome and host—especially newer residents. Show them around town. Give advice on places to eat, shop, and play in your area. Introduce them to your church family.

Be on the lookout for that lone person at your church.

Invite them to go eat after the service or hang out with them during the week.

4. Pay attention to people's needs, likes, and concerns

Surprise guests with their favorite food or beverage. Supply them with material items they need. These little touches will leave a lasting impression on your guests. It doesn't need to be anything pricey, just a thoughtful touch to show that you care.

These are great pathways into further conversations. Pay attention to the deeper heart issues: a person's fears, dreams, hopes, and questions. Let's learn how to "answer each person" (Col. 4:2) rather than giving rote presentations.

5. Don't feel the need to copy others' practices

My wife currently hosts a monthly book club at our house. This is not a "Christian book club," but a group of ladies from our neighborhood reading popular books together. They eat and talk about the monthly selection.

I coach baseball, and this has allowed me to hang out with many dads. Perhaps you can cook. Perhaps you need to learn!

Whatever you do, do it with gospel intentionality and cultural sensibility. Densely urban areas will differ from suburban areas. Dangerous areas will differ from safer ones. Do good, contextual hospitality.

6. Greet warmly, engage sincerely, say goodbye thoughtfully

The greetings and farewells in the New Testament have always struck me (Acts 20:36; 21:5–6; Rom. 16:16). They are filled with warmth, love, and meaning.

When someone comes into your home, greet them affectionately. Take their coat. Offer them a drink. Give them a place to sit.

As you talk with people, ask about their life. Don't turn everything back on yourself. Put your phone away. Draw attention to Jesus's grace.

When they're ready to leave, walk them to the door, or

even to their car. Invite them back. All of these gestures convey value and love. And people remember them.

Be a Good Guest

You'll learn to show good hospitality by learning to receive it. Be thankful for people's generosity. Write the host a thank-you note or an email to express your gratitude. Hospitality flows out of a humble, grateful heart.

Be a student of hospitality when hosted. You will grow in hospitality as you seek to humbly learn from others.

Finally, meditate on the goodness of God. We were the orphan, but God adopted us into his family. We were the stranger without a country, but we have been brought into the kingdom. We were the widow, but Jesus has become our Groom. We were the poor, but we now have a glorious inheritance. We are pilgrims here on earth, but Jesus has gone to prepare a place for us. Marvel regularly at this grace, and remember that the proper response to God's grace is grace—a lifetime of gratitude, generosity, and hospitality.

24

THE DIFFERENCE BETWEEN GOOD LEADERS AND GREAT LEADERS

Noel Heikkinen

In my late teens and early 20s, I was an arrogant young punk. I thought I knew everything about the Christian faith and how ministry was supposed to work. I had ideas, dreams, and, of course, verses.

For several years, I bounced around between various churches and college ministries looking for something I didn't know I was missing—until I found it: men excited about training younger men.

Over the past two decades of ministry, I've observed many young guys who remind me of my former self. They bounce from church to church, probably unsure of exactly what they're looking for.

Here's what I think helps to explain it: Bad leaders *repel* young leaders, good leaders *raise up* young leaders, and great leaders *launch* young leaders.

Bad Leaders Repel

Young leaders usually think they're looking for a *place* to lead. If they can just find that church or organization where they "fit," then they'll flourish. But what young leaders are really looking for—whether they know it or not—is a *person* who will help them learn how to lead.

Leadership in the church—and especially in the work of church planting—is not gleaned by osmosis. It won't just "happen." It takes older leaders intentionally pouring their lives into younger ones. Paul told Timothy to "teach others" what Paul had taught him (2 Tim. 2:2). To raise up young leaders, you don't need a big leadership program; you need an intentional life.

When an older leader is insecure, he's unlikely to keep alongside a younger leader who challenges his way of doing things. The older leader sees these challenges as an affront to his preferred methods and systems.

On the flip side, an older leader who doesn't know how to lead will often abdicate to a younger leader too quickly, thus violating Paul's warning to "not be hasty in the laying on of hands" (1 Tim. 5:22).

Both approaches will eventually cause the young leader to bail, get frustrated with ministry, or burn out.

Good Leaders Raise Up

Good leaders recognize talent in younger people and are excited about the opportunity to train the next generation. They create or adopt plans and systems to mentor with the skills these young people need.

Unfortunately, things often stall here, since many older leaders fail to take the crucial next step that great leaders know they must take. It's not enough to identify and train young leaders; older leaders must let them *lead*. This means giving them responsibility in specific areas.

Older leaders who only delegate responsibility on the basis of fully developed skill will never delegate responsibility. Leadership development means trusting younger leaders even though they won't do it as well as you could (at least initially).

Great Leaders Launch

After spending years mentoring and training me as a leader, the pastors at my church noticed I was bouncing off the glass ceiling of our organization. So they did something few older leaders are willing to do: they opened a skylight in the glass ceiling to launch me farther than they had gone. Giving younger leaders opportunities to surpass you in ministry takes profound humility, wrought only by the Spirit of God.

From my experience with these godly men, here are a few ways you can launch young leaders:

- Give them a chance to lead (and not just when you are on vacation). If they are an up-and-coming preacher, give them a prime spot in the preaching rotation and sit in the front row, listening attentively and taking notes.
- Be their biggest public cheerleader. Encourage them in their strengths in front of those who are watching.
- Be their behind-the-scenes coach. Help them learn to face their weaknesses and apply the gospel to their own soul. This is crucial for anyone who desires to lead others.
- If they are a church planter, encourage them to take anyone they can convince to go with them. Give them permission—even encouragement—to poach your best people.

None of this is easy. It takes humble dependence on the Good Shepherd (John 10). But that's the greatest leadership trait I've learned from the men who trained me. They were, and continue to be, the most humble servant leaders I've ever met. I know this because they are still on the pastoral team I now lead.

That was never the plan. In fact, they did all this work with the intention of launching me to plant a new church.

The biggest reason I stayed, instead of planting a church, is because we had a good team. Together, we hope to train hundreds of young men to plant churches all over the globe.

And now, I'm trusting God to eventually provide the leader who can take the church farther than I could ever dream. At that point, it'll be my turn to fade quietly into the background.

25

HOW TO (NOT) OVERBURDEN PEOPLE IN YOUR CHURCH PLANT

Aaron Weiss

Church planting requires tenacity. Ask anyone who's done it, and they'll tell you the responsibility of planting and leading a church is a heavy load. A joyful one, to be sure, but weighty too.

Because of this, church planters are prone to overburden their congregations. It's easy to misjudge what level of involvement or responsibility members should have. With the sheer magnitude of things to be done, it's hard to know how much to call members to do.

For some, being involved in a church-planting team will be attractive because of the obvious need. These early adopters can be wonderful supports. And yet, this same sense of urgency may repel others from what seems to be an overwhelming task.

I've had several friends tell me, "We could never attend a church plant. It's just too much work." At one level, I get it. Planting a church is costly, and it's right that people feel that cost. Indeed, the costliness will likely root out those looking for an easy ride in the Christian life (as if there is such a thing; Mark 8:34–35).

But that doesn't eliminate the danger of overloading members of church-planting teams with undue burdens. When there is so much to do, how do we develop and empower people without burning them out?

Vital to any church's health is encouraging and

developing God's people for service. But it can prove harmful if the expectations given come (1) too fast, (2) are too much, or (3) are too heavy for them to carry.

Too Fast

It's easy to overload people by expecting significant contributions too quickly. Developing disciples takes time. Note Paul's instruction to Timothy about the qualifications of an elder: "If someone does not know how to manage his own household, how will he care for God's church?" (1 Tim. 3:5). Intrinsic to the point Paul makes here is that spiritual leadership within the church is developed in the everyday rhythms of faithful discipleship, and is thus evidenced over time.

In the case of elders, we mustn't make the mistake of loading the spiritual leadership of a church on unprepared shoulders. Having experienced the pain of placing good people into leadership positions too early has taught me the importance of investing in ongoing rhythms of development and incremental growth.

In short, many church planters would do well to *slow down.*

God gives believers the gifts of the Spirit to equip and edify, so that the works of ministry are shared as the Spirit has apportioned (1 Cor. 12:4–8). So as believers mature, they will grow in their capacity to contribute. Don't expect the spiritual newborns in your church family to contribute like the spiritual parents and grandparents. This may delay some of your plans, but it will pay off in the future.

Too Much

But what happens when your people are doing too much? Luke 10:38–42 tells of two sisters who hosted Jesus in their home. Martha, who was "distracted with much serving," grows frustrated with her sister Mary, who elects to remain with Jesus instead of doing chores. So Martha interrupts Jesus: "Tell her to help me!"

Similarly, it's possible for some in church plants to view others as less committed due to their lack of activity. Jesus's response to Martha addresses us all: "Martha,

Martha, you are anxious and troubled about many things, but one thing is necessary. Mary has chosen the good portion, which will not be taken away from her" (Luke 10:41–42). Far from an excuse to sit back and let others do the work for us, this story exhorts us to remember that the work is not the ultimate aim. Jesus is.

Consider the load your people are carrying. Is it drawing them away from Jesus? We don't want our people to miss out on the best thing because they were overloaded with too many commitments and responsibilities.

A friend and fellow church planter once told me to "pastor the church Jesus has given you." As a young leader eager for rapid growth, this was timely advice. My church was neither a labor force for "my vision" nor mere bait to attract more people. My church was the people I was summoned to love.

If you're overworked, reassess. Wearing an overloaded backpack seems fine until you're required to climb a mountain with it. Can your church afford ministry staff for overloaded volunteers? Can you kill any programs, or streamline any ministries, to lessen the load? Think creatively: Are there ways you can partner with other churches or share resources to accomplish more together? If you've come from a mother church, guard your heart against stubborn angularity. Ask for help in areas of weakness. And don't forget to assess your heart: Is this a mission-critical component of your ministry, or something you can surrender for the health of your church?

Too Heavy

The third danger for church planters is overloading our congregations in *how* we lead. We may exhibit machismo for our exemplary dedication, and overburden those in our care by implicitly suggesting that real faith demands crushing commitment. It doesn't.

Sadly, my early experience of planting was marked by anxiety that this fledgling church may not make it or have any meaningful gospel influence. I took the full weight of the church on my shoulders—every success and failure became disproportionately personal. Needless to say, our church suffered as my unrealistic expectations stifled involvement. The load I carried was uninviting. It wasn't until late 2017 that I embraced a simple truth: If Jesus brought us to this community to plant a church for his name's sake, he will sustain it.

So we began to pray, "Lord, let our church's reputation be that *you* are building it."

If this prayer resonates with you, then stop carrying the load that was never yours to carry. Jesus is inviting you into his work to accomplish *his* purposes, not yours. Transfer your burdens to him, and find rest for your soul (Matt. 11:28–30).

26

WHY YOUR CHURCH PLANT SHOULD EMBRACE PLURAL LEADERSHIP

Tony Merida

When you talk about church structure, my friend Ryan Townsend says that it's kind of like talking about the plumbing at your house. No one comes over to see it, but everyone notices if it's broken. And broken plumbing can lead to a big, embarrassing mess!

My 19-year-old Ukrainian-born son, James, may be the exception to this rule. He loves to fix things, and he enjoys pointing out problems in people's homes—often unsolicited. We recently commissioned him to go help his aunt and uncle get their house ready to sell. Upon arrival, James texted us: "Lots of problems. Plumbing. Expensive."

Healthy Foundation

That's a pretty good description of some church structures. Problems abound. Many of which come from a lack of healthy church eldership and membership. And when it comes to changing these foundational issues down the road, it can be costly, painful, and overwhelming.

In our pastoral intern program at our church, we spend significant time on "plumbing." We want our guys to have deep convictions about eldership and membership, and even be ready to pay the price to implement these things.

Building a healthy church structure is hard work—

harder than crafting a clever vision statement or coming up with a cool church name. But it's far more important. It's hard work because it requires thorough assessments, long conversations, clear communication, a willingness to let go of control (especially if you're viewed as the "senior leader"), a willingness to be challenged, and more. But it's needed, and it's worth it.

We want our church planters to get excited about biblical leadership structure, not for the sake of structure itself, but so that the church can be both *missional* and *pastoral*. Your structure can either help or hinder (1) how the flock is cared for and (2) how the church lives on mission.

From Pyramid to Plurality

We planted our church with a plurality of elders. I wanted to avoid the "pastor and his staff" model that has one guy atop the pyramid. We wanted a plurality of elders/pastors caring for and mobilizing the congregation, under the leadership of the true senior pastor, Jesus Christ, who alone sits atop the pyramid.

We don't even want to plant a church unless we have more than one pastor. We often tell aspiring planters, *who* you plant with is more important than *where* you plant. In other words, team is more important than location. Under most circumstances, I believe one can endure and thrive in any location with the right team.

Further, we need to shift our thinking on this profile more generally. For several years, "the man" was overplayed in church planting. The idea was that, in order to be a church planter, you needed to be an alpha male, Enneagram 3 macho-man. Hopefully we can see the problems with such an idea.

I long for a revival of awareness that emphasizes the need for a team of people to plant a church well—composed of missional men and women, and shepherded by a plurality of humble, wise, godly pastors. I believe this will fuel the planting of healthy churches in every nook and cranny of the globe.

Valuing Plurality

We find numerous examples of plural eldership in the New Testament. Elders are seen in the churches of Judea and the surrounding area (Acts 11:30; James 5:14–15); in Jerusalem (Acts 15; 21); in Derbe, Lystra, and Antioch (Acts 14:20–23); in Ephesus (Acts 20; 1 Tim. 5:17–25); and in Northwest Asia Minor (1 Pet. 1:1; 5:1). (It's interesting, by the way, that while many challenge the notion of a plurality of elders/pastors, no one seems to advocate for a single deacon model. We need a plurality of both.) Acts 14 is crucial for church planters. Before Paul and Barnabas returned to Antioch, from their first so-called missionary journey, Paul returned to strengthen the souls of the disciples. What did he and Barnabas do on this return trip?

> When they had preached the gospel to that city and had made many disciples, they returned to Lystra and to Iconium and to Antioch, strengthening the souls of the disciples, encouraging them to continue *in the faith,* and saying that through many tribulations we must enter the kingdom of God. And when *they had appointed elders for them in every church, with prayer and fasting they committed them to the Lord* in whom they had believed. (Acts 14:21–23, emphasis added)

How can Paul feel good enough about a church to leave it to exist without him? What did he want to have in place? Notice the three foundations: (1) apostolic instruction—"the faith"; (2) pastoral oversight—this is the first appearance of elders in Gentile churches, and what occurs seems to set the trend for what becomes the norm; and (3) prayerful trust in God.

Parity and Plurality

I'd like to offer one final consideration to those already bought into this model, and it pertains to the "first among equals" idea. For some who have plurality, their elders operate like a board. They're not shepherds. I don't recommend this approach. Others see their elders as pastors, but there's a hierarchy in authority and/or importance. I'm not a fan of this either. I'm for a team of pastors who have equal authority and importance. We recognize that not all elders are equal in gifting, biblical knowledge, and experience—1 Timothy 5:17 indicates this in regard to teaching. But there's more to shepherding than teaching and preaching.

For many who advocate for the "first among equals" model, however, the inherent assumption is that one pastor is better at every shepherding issue or has more authority over every issue. To such thinking, I'd want to ask, "Why do you assume that the guy who's more capable in teaching will also be more gifted at care-giving, counseling, administrating, or mobilizing?" These are vital aspects of shepherding, too.

But how does this actually work? Don't you have to have a "first among equals"? At our church, we say this: We have a first among equals depending on the issue. Here are some essentials for making that happen:

- *Humility and trust.* If you're a control freak, this won't work.
- *Patience and self-control.* You may not like the pace at which things happen in plurality.
- *Love.* You have to bear with one another in love; you'll know each other's flaws as well as anyone else in the church.
- *Being quick to listen, slow to speak, and slow to anger.* You don't have to voice a strong opinion about everything.
- *Respect for one another.* You have to value the perspectives of everyone.
- *An awareness of each other's strengths.* This is essential in order to know when and how to defer to each other.

So in our efforts to plant churches, let's not just seek to plant churches—let's seek to plant healthy churches, led by a healthy team of pastors, for the good of the church and the advancement of the mission. This will require us to give due consideration to this less celebrated aspect of church planting.

27

CLOSED ON SUNDAY: CELEBRATING EASTER IN THE SHADOW OF GLOBAL DEATH

Doug Ponder

For the first—and hopefully last—time in our lives, churches around the world are about to celebrate Easter by *not* gathering on Sunday.[25] It's a tragic picture of these sad and scary days. Yet it's similar in several ways to what happened on the first Easter Sunday.

John shows us Mary Magdalene weeping outside the tomb (John 20:11), while Matthew adds that she and the other Mary were very afraid (Matt. 28:4). The disciples, meanwhile, were so scared they stayed indoors in a group small enough to satisfy the coronavirus quarantine (John 20:19).

But then Jesus showed up, and everything began to change. To the two Marys Jesus said, "Do not be afraid" (Matt. 28:9), and to the disciples he declared, "Peace be with you" (John 20:21). The risen Christ is still speaking these words to his people—church planters included. He sees the struggle of your disrupted rhythms. He knows your fears about the survival of your church and the well-being of your staff, whose livelihoods are wed to the generosity of his people. And he knows the added pressure you feel even now as Easter Sunday approaches: What will

---

[25] This article was originally published on April 8, 2020, when the COVID-19 pandemic was rapidly spreading around the world.

you do? How will you help your people celebrate good news in such hard times?

In view of the diversity of churches and ministerial contexts, there is probably no "one-size-fits-all" approach to celebrating Easter during COVID-19. But here are four words of exhortation derived from the first Easter Sunday, from the nature of the church itself, and from the promises of our Lord.

1. Don't Give in to the Pressure to Perform

Easter is a celebration of what Christ has done, not a demonstration of what a church can do. This is true every Sunday, but it's essential we remember this now. That's because the routine pressures of our weekly preparation have become prime territory for our Enemy's work. If you're livestreaming services, you may especially feel the added pressure to do something fantastic or memorable, or at least "not boring."

Don't give in to the pressure to perform. Instead, remember that Sunday services are not about manufacturing a certain experience, but faithfully holding Jesus forth to people who need to see him (John 12:21). The church is not, and never has been, a show. So, rather than fretting about the quality of your streaming service, count it all joy that such measures are a cheap substitute for the real thing: the *ekklesia*, the assembly of God's gathered ones.

2. Don't Downplay Easter's Significance

If one group is prone to overemphasizing Easter in all the wrong ways, another is prone to underemphasizing holy days for the opposite reason. Indeed, it's tempting to soothe sorrows over the present circumstances by saying, "It's just another Sunday, after all." But I would caution you against this, for such a sentiment betrays a common tendency to downplay the means of grace. And while it's true, in one sense, that every Sunday after the resurrection is "mini-Easter," there are still good reasons why the church has given the resurrection a full season of its own (Eastertide).

Instead of downplaying Easter, acknowledge that—as with so many things in a sin-stained world—this is not the way it's supposed to be. Then lead your people, like Israel in captivity (Ps. 137), to long for a return to corporate worship. We should value gathering so much that missing Easter makes us feel the losses of this present moment all the more.

3. Rejoice Even as You Lament

Matthew tells us that the women who first learned of Jesus's resurrection "departed quickly from the tomb with fear and great joy" (Matt. 28:8). I've always liked this unexpected combination of emotions. Joy (obviously) because they'd just discovered that Jesus is alive, but also fear (presumably) because they weren't sure how every detail would work out. Similarly, Easter is a reminder that we have much to rejoice about.

Sin and death have been defeated and will one day be destroyed (1 Cor. 15:54–57). Yet we still experience the sting of death, as COVID-19 painfully reminds us. If ever there were an Easter when we might feel fear and sadness in the midst of great joy, it's now. So let us lead our people to celebrate accordingly, rejoicing in what Christ has accomplished already, even as we lament the "not yet" and long for that day when death can touch us no more.

4. Rest in the One Still at Work

On his best days, a planter is so confident in Jesus's promise to build the church that he's willing to sell everything he owns and move across the country (or the world) to start a church with just his family, his Bible, and a half-baked dream. But on his worst days, a pastor is wracked with worry. This anxiety comes from feeling and acting like *everything depends on me.*

For however long the church is prohibited from gathering, pastors and planters have been handed a unique gift (à la Gen. 50:20). Most of the platforms and programs that prop up our false sense of security have been removed. We've been left with virtually nothing but Jesus himself.

Instead of resisting this state of affairs, let's rest in the One who's still with his people by the Spirit, through the Word and in prayer. For if we can trust him with our own lives, shouldn't we trust him with the life of the church he bought with his own blood? So don't just preach a message *about* Easter this week. Practice the *meaning* of Easter, too: Christ is risen indeed, so you can rest in him.

28

GROWING ELDERS IN YOUR CHURCH PLANT: A GRADUAL STRATEGY

Yancey Arrington

Many churches create a culture that revolves around their pastor. He's expected to preach all sermons, mediate every dispute, oversee each program, and generally make all the decisions. I call this the "pastor-centered church." If you plant this kind of church, it will likely be destined for failure because even if you somehow avoid burnout, eventually you'll relocate, retire, or die, leaving behind a church that feels abandoned.

But healthy church plants understand the apostle Paul's instructions to Timothy to find faithful men who can share the leadership of the church (2 Tim. 2:1–2). Church planting is not about being "the man," but finding and training "the men" who will lead with you at the elder level.

After establishing church plants, Paul demonstrated a process whereby elders were appointed. For example, in Titus 1:5, the apostle's strategy for Crete was for Titus to "put what remained into order, and appoint elders in every town." Initially, these church plants existed without a body of elders. While we don't know exactly how much time elapsed, we do know selecting elders came later. And it came slowly.

Prematurely establishing elders can not only handicap your church's development, but reverse it, resulting in failure. Perhaps this is why Paul counsels Timothy to "not be hasty" in establishing elders (1 Tim. 5:22). It's critical to get right and disastrous to get wrong.

So, what's a young church planter to do? Let me offer a three-stage strategy planters can implement which provides a gradual progression of leadership which might not begin with an elder body, but definitely ends with one.

Stage One: Lone Elder

This first phase is essential in both promoting and protecting your church's unique DNA. You hold the vision, values, and strategy for your plant. In this initial season, everything concerning those areas runs through you.

This doesn't mean a lone elder doesn't have any accountability. He absolutely must! Many planters at this stage create an advisory board of godly men (often other pastors and church leaders outside the congregation) who regularly meet with him and select staff throughout the year.

It's also during this time that you're looking for men who have the potential to become elders. You spend much of your time investing in those relationships to discern if any might make good elders in the future (calling, competence, chemistry). After you begin forming your church's elder body by inviting, training, and deploying qualified men to serve as elders, you move into Stage Two.

Stage Two: Lead Elder

During this stage, as the lead elder among elders, you're still at the front of your church's decision-making process in matters of doctrine, discipline, and direction. This gives your new elder team time to see how their lead pastor operates and to notice his strengths and weaknesses.

At Stage Two, you might call the plays while the elder team helps execute them. This doesn't mean the team can't disagree with you. It also doesn't mean they can't outvote you. However, it's very clear at this stage that the lead pastor is the "first among equals," whereby the team is heavily following your lead.

Think of Stage Two as the ministerial equivalent of "teaching someone to fish" in the age-old leadership maxim. I believe this phase can often take several years because you aren't just trying to grow as a team, but as a brotherhood, and brotherhoods are forged over time. And when you feel like you've got a team of brothers who've been properly forged, then it's time to move to the last phase.

Stage Two: Lead Elders

Stage Three has the kind of team composed of men who could lead their own congregations. They stay because they're here for the long haul, to make disciples in their community through the local church.

In Stage Three, there's a blurring of lines concerning roles and responsibilities between the lead pastor and his team. There may be an elder responsible for pastoral care, another for the preaching ministry, still another for the oversight of ministries, with none of them being the founding pastor. In this stage, the lead pastor should be able to more acutely focus his time on his passion points and ministry strengths.

Brothers be warned, Stage Three demands you die to yourself in ways that might be harder than you imagine. This is where we must strangle that ego which often prevents some lead pastors from enduring in ministry as well as their congregations from having structural and spiritual health. Let's not risk our churches with a strategy that can handicap the growth of aspiring leaders around us.

As a church matures, so should its leadership model. While Stage Three is the place we would never start our church plant, it's the place we must finish. A church planter isn't just *the* pastor, he must be about the development of *other* pastors on his staff. The health of his church and future church plants depends upon it.

29

THE DANGEROUS DESIRE FOR CHURCH GROWTH

Adam Ramsey

Every church planter begins with a desire for his church to grow. And yet, what can often be missed—even as we come hurtling out of the gates with all our plans, prayers, and strategies—is the deadly desire to build our own empire. This kind of desire for church growth, if left unchecked, will have catastrophic results.

There is a type of desire for church growth that has the capacity to prove deadly to you, your family, and your church, because its driving motivations are worldly.

There is a ministry mindset that looks and sounds impressive—one that potentially even uses all the right gospel terminology—but as you get closer, the scent is unmistakable. It smells of Babel (Gen. 11:1–9).

Motives Matter

In his book *The Imperfect Pastor*, Zack Eswine speaks to the explosive potential of desire in church leaders: "Desire is a firework. Handled wisely it fills the night sky with light, color, beauty, and delight. Handle desire poorly, and it can burn your neighborhood down."[26]

As a church planter and pastor, I have to make war every day on ego and impatience, while breathing the toxic air of a wider church culture that readily applauds quick

---

[26] Zack Eswine, *The Imperfect Pastor: Discovering Joy in Our Limitations through a Daily Apprenticeship with Jesus* (Crossway, 2015), 19.

results over godly longevity. Delusions of my own giftedness and feelings of inadequacy take turns competing for my heart's attention. And that's just Monday morning.

The battle is real. And so is the tragic reality that many church plants, for a variety of reasons, just don't make it. This often results in church planters feeling pressured to grow quickly in order to survive the infancy stages of a new church.

But when producing results comes at the expense of building on a gospel foundation with gospel motivations, we may as well be trying to erect skyscrapers on frozen lakes.

Attach your identity to your achievements, and the outcome will be as predictable as it is avoidable. Whether it's the heat of trials, or a season where the church plant plateaus, or the erosion of your competence to produce impressive results; when the frozen ice of a misplaced identity melts away, the result is catastrophe. Every single time (Prov. 16:18).

It may take months or it may go on for decades, but eventually the unchecked ego will crack the ice, and the falling debris will hit everyone involved.

Lesson from Dr. Seuss

As we prayerfully consider what our future church plant may look like, we (rightly) dream of a growing, fruit-bearing, multiplying church. And what pastor doesn't want that? The danger comes when we believe God *owes* us that church. When we start thinking ministry success is something we *deserve* for all our efforts. When we become like Dr. Seuss's Yertle the Turtle, supposing our gifts are under-utilized in the sphere of kingdom influence we've currently been assigned.

Do you remember how subtle the creep of ambition and entitlement were in the heart of the turtle king? The story starts like this:

> *On the far-away island of Sala-ma-Sond, Yertle the Turtle was king of the pond.*
> *A nice little pond. It was clean. It was neat. The water*

was warm. There was plenty to eat.
The turtles had everything turtles might need. And they were all happy. Quite happy indeed.
They were . . . until Yertle, the king of them all, decided the kingdom he ruled was too small.
"I'm ruler," said Yertle, "of all that I see. But I don't see enough. That's the trouble with me.
With this stone for a throne, I look down on my pond, but I cannot look down on the places beyond.
This throne that I sit on is too, too low down. It ought to be higher!" he said with a frown.
"If I could sit high, how much greater I'd be! What a king! I'd be ruler of all that I see!"

– Theodor Geisel (Dr. Seuss)[27]

Yertle is the epitome of entitlement. Those he was called to *serve* were turned into a platform from which he could be *seen*. And the results were, predictably, catastrophic. But what is perhaps most scary about Yertle is that the size of the pond is irrelevant. Yertles can exist in a puddle or the Pacific Ocean. Yertles can exist in core groups of 20 or megachurches of 20,000.

Allure of Ambition

Brennan Manning once warned that "ambition to be a star in the body of Christ is alluring and seductive; it is also demonic, the glamorous enemy of all servanthood and love."[28] At the top of the staircase of self-exalting ambition is not a crown, but a noose. If Haman can teach church planters anything, it is that those who exalt themselves usually end up hanging from the noose of their own success (Esth. 7:9–10).

Standing in contrast is the humble example of the incarnate Savior. We follow in the footsteps of Christ, who "came not to be served but to serve" (Mark 10:45). We must refuse to pimp out his bride for our own applause.

---

[27] Theodor Geisel (Dr. Seuss), *Yertle the Turtle and Other Stories* (Random House, Inc., 1958), 1–2.

[28] Brennan Manning, *A Glimpse of Jesus: The Stranger to Self-Hatred* (2003: HarperOne), 29,

If God calls us to plant or lead a church, let us remember that our pastoral influence does not exist to serve our dreams, but to serve God's people. Whatever platform Jesus gives us is not an opportunity to show off our gifts, but to show off his glory.

Much to Do, Nothing to Prove

None of this is to say that we shouldn't make goals, cultivate excellence in leadership gifts, or desire to see ministries grow. On the contrary, faithful stewardship is praised by Jesus (Matt. 25:20–21), and the godly aspiration for more people to know and delight in him is a Spirit-empowered desire at its root.

Though the two appear similar in many ways, the distinction between godly aspiration and worldly ambition is ultimately revealed in our willingness to be unseen. To receive none of the credit. To have every last bit of human applause fly over our heads to Christ.

Or let me phrase it another way, with a question I use to check my own heart: If God were to answer every one of my prayers for revival and renewal in my city—and he chose to do it primarily through *another* church—would I rejoice simply because he has done a great work? It's a question that humbles us, while reminding us of the eternal perspective we need in order to plant healthy churches. After all, don't we already possess the inheritance of infinite riches that comes from simply being God's child (Eph. 1:18–19)? In the words of Thomas Brooks, "Has not Christ given you himself? Is not one dram of his grace worth more than ten thousand worlds? Why, then, should you envy the gifts he gives others?"[29]

This is what the gospel declares to us: While we are owed nothing, in Christ we have received everything. And because of that reality, we can give ourselves to planting, shepherding, and serving churches with everything we have (1 Cor. 15:10).

Pastor, remember this: You belong to Jesus. You have much to do, and nothing to prove.

---

[29] Thomas Brooks, ed. by C. H. Spurgeon, *Smooth Stones from Ancient Brooks* (London: Forgotten Books Publishing, 2012), 149.

30

WHY CHURCH-PLANTING SUCCESS IS DANGEROUS

Matt Hodges

Last summer, I took a 10-week sabbatical. If you'd asked me at the time why I was taking it, I could've listed a number of reasons, all of which were legitimate and sincere. But what I didn't expect was how God would use my sabbatical to teach me a single foundational truth. I wish I could grab every church planter by the face, look into their eyes, and tell them: *Your joy must be rooted* in *Jesus, not in doing things* for *Jesus.*

Having gone through the throes of planting a church—the time, energy, and effort it took just to keep our heads above water—the line between my walk *with* Jesus and my ministry *for* Jesus was often blurred.

And I came to realize that my identity was more tied to doing things for the kingdom than it was in being a son welcomed into it. This led to an unnoticed, dangerous shift in my heart: At some point I traded being sustained by communion with God for the recognition I received for serving him.

Be Careful with Success

By external measures, our plant was a "success." And while we knew this was largely in spite of our efforts, the accomplishments felt good.

And what the heart loves, the mind will justify.

So justify it did.

- *It's good to want to do "big things for God." After all, it's for God.*
- *I'm not seeking to build my platform; I'm seeking to build God's.*
- *It's not my renown I'm after; it's God's.*

During my sabbatical, God began uprooting these refrains and exposing them for what they really were: joy-stealing rationalizations that were actually less concerned with God glorifying *himself*, and more concerned with *me* being the one he used to do so.

Stepping away from the platform and the responsibilities forced me to evaluate whether Jesus was the means or the end. I was even off of social media, which allowed me to realize that the old adage of a tree falling in the woods could be aptly retooled to: "If you have an edifying encounter with the Lord in his Word, but don't post a picture or tweet a profound reflection, did it really happen?"

Beware of "Serving" God

I discovered that my language of "being used by God" or "making an impact for the kingdom" (good things in and of themselves, certainly) was often nothing more than a veiled attempt to baptize my own ambitions.

In *The Imperfect Pastor*, Zack Eswine recalls realizations from his own testimony that rang painfully true for me: "I did not know yet that serving God could be used, even by me, as a means to try, in line with the Serpent's old whisper, to become like God." And, "It is possible for ministry leaders to desire greatness in ways no different from anyone, anywhere in our culture. Attaching Jesus's name to these desires doesn't change the fact that they look just like the cravings of the world."[30]

By attaching spiritual language to my accolades, I could convince myself and others I wasn't in it for the glory. It was as if the desire for platform and influence was okay because it was "religious." But this is precisely what Jesus exposed in the Pharisees:

---

[30] Zack Eswine, *The Imperfect Pastor: Discovering Joy in Our Limitations through a Daily Apprenticeship with Jesus* (Crossway, 2015), 20, 30.

> You search the Scriptures because you think that in them you have eternal life; and it is they that bear witness about me, yet you refuse to come to me that you may have life. . . . How can you believe, when you receive glory from one another and do not seek the glory that comes from the only God? (John 5:39, 44)

From an external perspective, no one served God like the Pharisees did. They were masters of Scripture who dedicated their lives to teaching and enforcing God's law. But Jesus saw through their religious masks. He knew they craved praise and recognition from their fellow man—and serving God was a convenient means to that end.

Church planting can leave us particularly vulnerable to this temptation. For one, it's easy to draw a correlation—even causation—between our own abilities and the "success" of the church we planted. On top of that, our people are susceptible to being drawn to a single personality. It's a perfect recipe for the Enemy to spoon-feed our ego.

Behold the True Treasure

We don't need to adopt a false humility that refuses to either recognize our gifts or be grateful God's chosen to use them. But it does mean we must be on high alert to the possibility that what we really want, like the Pharisees, is "glory from one another."

We need to ask hard questions, such as: *If God would still get the glory, but the notoriety was taken from me specifically, would I be satisfied? If there would be just as much of an "impact" made for the kingdom, but I don't get noticed, would I be okay? If I give my life over to toil that's rarely recognized, but I have deep fellowship with Jesus, would that be enough for me?*

Because if Jesus himself isn't enough, we will turn serving him into a means of usurping him. Our ministry will become a way of satiating our need to be noticed and affirmed. And what follows, tragically, is that the people with whom we're entrusted become pawns in that game, pieces to be strategically moved and manipulated to maximize our platform—instead of God's beloved children for whom we'll give an account (Heb. 13:17).

Like the religious leaders in Jesus's day, we'll end up trading true fellowship with God for a facade of religious activity and accomplishment. But Jesus *is* enough. Hence his insistence on where true life is found (John 5:40).

The kingdom of heaven is like a treasure hidden in a field—a treasure worth giving up everything for—including the accolades and recognition of ministry. The temporary high of receiving praise pales in comparison to the deep, lasting joy that only communion with Christ can bring.

And when that truth sinks in, we'll be free to follow in our Lord's path—a path of selfless obscurity, quietly serving and pointing people to the glory and grace of the Father.

31

CHURCH PLANTER, REDEFINE SUCCESS AND SEEK EMOTIONAL HEALTH

Tyler St. Clair

"Can you brothers pray for me? I'm mentally, physically, and emotionally depleted from pushing all week despite being sick. I'm so discouraged I don't even want to go to our gathering today, let alone preach."

This was a text I sent a few dear brothers several weeks ago. Gripped by anxiety and physically zapped, I sat in my car and sobbed uncontrollably an hour before our worship gathering began. I'd hit a wall. Most church-planting training doesn't prepare you for these moments.

Don't get me wrong: Most training I know about is solid and robust. But as I've planted a church, I've been faced with challenges that have taken a toll on my emotional well-being. *How do I process the pain of betrayal or having my trust broken? Whom do I confide in about pastoral issues? Who will shepherd my soul amid stress and difficulties while I'm learning to lead?*

I believe the lack of attention given to emotional health in church planting has yielded a culture where we ignore or downplay certain issues—until a brother falls into sin, when we're all forced to step back and ask: *Why?*

We mustn't underestimate the emotional costs involved in planting a church. Whether it be the constant change, pervasive uncertainty, isolation, support raising and recruiting, leadership development, frenetic pace, or unrealistic expectations—church planters need to manage all of these, not to mention the daily responsibility to lead people in the truth.

Redefining Success

Many look at the size, scale, and number of services to evaluate "success." Perhaps one of the main reasons many church planters crumble inwardly is because they've bought into these false assessments of true success. Some (myself included) observe the ministries or gifts God has given to others, compare ourselves, and then are driven to doubt and despair.

I've spoken with countless planters who are discouraged because they feel their churches don't measure up. And I believe many are driven to despair in part because "bigger" and "faster" have eclipsed *faithfulness* as our ultimate aim. Or more subtly, the assumption becomes that these things are the fruit of faithfulness. But this could not be further from the truth:

> I have fought the good fight, I have finished the race, I have kept the faith. There is reserved for me the crown of righteousness, which the Lord, the righteous Judge, will give me on that day, and not only to me, but to all who have loved his appearing. (2 Tim. 4:7–8)

Imagine Paul evaluating his ministry as we often do. If size and speed had been his metrics for success, then ending up in prison would have been the utmost failure, and surely no reason to rejoice. But rejoice he did (Phil. 1:18–19). So instead of growing despondent because of what we don't have, what if we praised God for uniquely equipping us for our church-planting task?

Planting through Pain

Pain and church planting are inevitably intertwined. Paul's ministry was marked by being "afflicted, perplexed, persecuted, and struck down" (2 Cor. 4:8–9). While on my planting journey, I've watched many men, and their wives, wrestle with depression and anxiety.

So how should we respond to the emotional pain we face?

I'd suggest at least three ways. These are not exhaustive, but I believe they can help.

1. Acknowledge

King David was candid about his pain. Instead of ignoring his heart, he expressed his loneliness, sorrow, and discouragement (Ps. 25:16; 31:10; 42:5; 69:29).

First and foremost, we need to acknowledge our experience before the Lord—as David did—with raw honesty and humble trust.

2. Embrace Frailty

When Paul told the Corinthians "we have this treasure in jars of clay," he was embracing frailty. Why? "To show that the surpassing power belongs to God and not to us" (2 Cor. 4:7).

I've experienced things inwardly I thought I'd never feel. I've felt worry from unrealistic expectations. I've known sorrow and loneliness due to the weight of shepherding people in dark places and being the lead pastor in a small church plant. I've felt the hurt of helping others who ended up turning on me and my family.

But even still, so much of my pain comes from relying on my own strength. I need to repent, embrace my weakness, and take comfort as I rest in God's power—accepting my limits instead of attempting to surpass them. God's power is not manifested in our competence and capability. Rather, he displays his surpassing power precisely because, in and of ourselves, we are neither competent nor capable.

3. Don't Fly Solo

All difficulties are exacerbated when suffering alone. I know many pastors who scream "community" but are personally isolated. Planter, your heart needs tending and care. Find godly men who will bandage the wounds of your soul before you spiritually bleed out. As Dietrich Bonhoeffer aptly noted, "[Man] needs his brother solely because of Jesus Christ. The Christ in his own heart is weaker than the Christ in the word of his brother; his own heart is uncertain, his brother's is sure."[31] Planting a church creates a uniquely dangerous opportunity for isolation. So pursue accountability. Don't let the pressure make you turn inward. Rather, ensure there are brothers and sisters who know you and will invest in you. Doing this will bless your family, your church, and your soul.

Emotional health is complex, and there's so much more that could be said. But the above three ways are foundational if we are to pursue humble dependence on Christ. And depending on him is far better than the size or "success" of any ministry.

After all, church planter, apart from him you can do nothing (John 15:5).

---

[31] Dietrich Bonhoeffer, *Life Together: A Discussion of Christian Fellowship* (Harper and Row Publishers, Inc., 1954), 23.

32

IF PAUL NEEDED FRIENDS, SO DO WE

Tony Merida

When surveying the life of the apostle Paul, we see his firm belief in the sufficiency of the gospel and his willingness to suffer for it. But there's another, often overlooked, feature of the Pauline mission: friendship. As Paul planted churches throughout the Roman world, he didn't do so as a one-man band.

Paul was relationally wealthy. He traveled with friends; he stayed with them; he visited them. He worked alongside them; he preached alongside them; he was beaten alongside them. He even sang in prison with friends. He encouraged them and was encouraged by them. At times, Paul disagreed with his friends. And at times, he reconciled with them.

A quick read through Acts shows Paul's commitment to, and genuine concern for, his friends: Barnabas, Titus, Silas, Luke, Priscilla, Aquilla, Lydia, Onesiphorus, Epaphroditus, John Mark, the Ephesian elders, and more.

In Romans 16, he mentions more than 30 names. The whole list oozes with affection; it also magnifies the gospel, demonstrates beautiful diversity (race, rank, gender), and contains moving expressions of honor.

In our gospel-centered movement, we should emphasize Paul's pattern of preaching the grace of Christ. But we should also highlight his deep commitment to friendship. Paul's constant interaction with his friends was a sign of maturity, not deficiency. Even the mighty apostle needed friends—and he needed them for the same reasons you do.

Here are three simple but glorious benefits of friendship.

1. Companionship

As people who image God, we were made for relationships. In the Garden of Eden, everything was glorious, everything "very good," except one thing: Adam was *alone*.

But wait—there's no sin yet. How could Adam need anything? He's in paradise! Why, then, was his heart aching? Tim Keller puts it well in his sermon "Spiritual Friendship":

> God made us in such a way that we couldn't even enjoy paradise without friends . . . Adam had a perfect quiet time every day for 24 hours a day. Yet he needed friends.[32]

We need friends because we are human beings, not trees. Our hearts ache when a friend or loved one has died. We miss their company. And when we're on our deathbeds, it won't be our accomplishments we long to hold (books, diplomas, trophies, house keys, and so on); we will want to hold people.

Don't let ministry—especially church planting—dehumanize you. You're more than a content producer. You're not the s*ermonator* who mechanically cranks out sermons. And church planting isn't lone ranger ministry, where you pioneer gospel work out on the barren frontier. We must value and cultivate friendships as people made in God's image.

2. Comfort

God regularly strengthens us through the presence and ministry of others. Consider Paul's statement about Titus: "For even when we came into Macedonia, our bodies had

---

[32] Timothy J. Keller, "Spiritual Friendship," sermon delivered on March 1, 1998, *The Gospel in Life*: https://gospelinlife.com/downloads/spiritual-friendship-6579/ accessed on Jan 29, 2021.

no rest, but we were afflicted at every turn—fighting without and fear within. But God, who comforts the downcast, comforted us by the coming of Titus" (2 Cor. 7:5–6). God used Titus to lift and strengthen Paul.

What do you need when you have "fighting without and fear within"? Friends. We need these kinds of friends because our hearts are fickle; because sin never sleeps; because Satan rages; and because the gospel is of first importance. We mustn't underestimate the importance of coming alongside one another in the fight of faith.

3. Joy

After sharing his vision to visit Rome, Paul tells the church of his desire to see them—in person. He's just written them a long letter, but he wants more: "I want to enjoy your company" (Rom. 15:24) and "be refreshed in your company" (Rom. 15:32). Even though Paul could communicate through writing, he knew that deeper joy and refreshment could only be experienced in person.

The apostle John says something similar: "Though I have much to write to you, I would rather not use paper and ink. Instead I hope to come to you and talk face to face, *so that our joy may be complete*" (2 John 12).

Don't settle for Facebook friends. We are holistic beings. You might be able to convey aspects of who you are online, but the online world will always fall short. The internet can't replace being physically present with people. We are people who feel, imagine, and react; we touch, move, and communicate through nonverbals.

We recently had our first "Gospel Party" with our church leaders. We invited everyone who has been sent out as a planter/pastor to come back and hang out for two days. It was so encouraging. We had friends on the back porch—laughing, playing, eating, praying, weeping, thinking, dreaming, planning, and worshiping. All of this was done together, and all of it was made possible through Jesus Christ, who is the friend of sinners like us.

Practice Friendship

So make time for your friends in the faith, your partners

in the gospel. Cultivate friendships in your own church. Show up in your various network or denominational meetings. Make a big deal out of "Titus ministry" (comforting fellow soldiers). May we seek to apply the various Proverbs that speak of friendship:

- Consistency: "A friend loves at all times, and a brother is born for adversity." (Prov. 17:17)
- Candor: "Faithful are the wounds of a friend; profuse are the kisses of an enemy" (Prov. 27:6).
- Compassion: "Whoever covers an offense seeks love, but he who repeats a matter separates close friends." (Prov. 17:9)

One of my favorite movie characters is Doc Holiday in *Tombstone.*[33] He's not a model of Christian piety, but there's one scene that has always moved me. Doc and Wyatt Earp are seeking to liberate an area from the "Cowboys," but Doc has grown ill with tuberculosis.

Nevertheless, out of love and loyalty, Doc rises from his deathbed to fight alongside Wyatt. In one solemn dialogue, Turkey Creek Jack Johnson asks, "Why are you doing this, Doc?" Doc replies, "Because Wyatt Earp is my friend."

Loyal gospel friends are priceless gifts from God. And they are made possible through our union with Christ, the ultimate Friend (John 15:15), who has covered our multitude of sins. May his grace to us flow from us in the practice of Christian friendship. And may we exalt the Friend of Sinners by planting churches.

---

[33] *Tombstone*, directed by George P. Cosmatos (Hollywood Pictures, 1993).

33

THE UNEXPECTED FRIENDSHIP THAT PREPARED ME FOR MINISTRY

David Doran Jr.

Barry called me every day for 11 years, usually more than once, sometimes up to 20 times a day. When Barry didn't call, I thought something might be up. When Barry didn't answer *my* call, I knew something was. After one particular day of radio silence, I went by Barry's apartment. It was on the ground floor, which meant I could bang on the windows when he didn't answer the door.

On this occasion, I glimpsed Barry huddled under a windowsill to stay out of my sight. Barry was 6'3″ and weighed 360 pounds, so he looked like a grizzly bear trying to hide behind a lampshade. I was filled with righteous indignation (at least that's how I justified it).

"I know you're using in there, Barry!" I yelled. "You can pretend you're not in there, but God is—he sees you right now! A holy God is in that apartment while you light up!" Barry responded, "You just don't understand, man. You don't know what I've been through and how hard it is."

It stings to admit I acted this way as a 23-year-old seminary student. I felt prophetic at the time, but I was a fool. I thought I was standing in Peter's line calling "Repent!" when in reality I was far closer to the Pharisee: "Thank God I'm not a sinner like this."

Only as I arrived to pick up Barry one Sunday morning did I begin to understand the depth of his struggle. I found him sprawled across the table with both arms gashed open, blood everywhere. Life was barely clinging to him. I called 911, and then lifted his arms above his head to slow the blood flow. As I hugged my dying friend, the depth of his pain was excruciatingly evident. Barry wasn't spending his days marking out dark plans for his next hit. The next hit was a mirage of relief. He was chasing an illusion of freedom—freedom from memories of abuse, from sins of the past, and from harsh realities of the present.

Friends on a Mission

Barry and I became friends when his first pastor called me. Barry needed distance from the trials and temptations of the neighborhood. The old bar around the corner and the old friend next door pose a challenging atmosphere to a young believer. Barry moved a couple miles away into my neighborhood—a long way when you ride the bus or walk—in order to create helpful space for new habits and relationships to grow.

Our friendship sprouted from God's Word. I would drop by and read the Bible with Barry. We'd read, talk, pray and then grab a bite at the deli down the street. Barry would try his most recent rap on me over a coney dog, or we'd throw a fishing line in the Detroit River to see if anything was biting.

Barry and I became partners in the gospel as the Spirit used our different gifts and strengths to help each other. Barry had a heart for the broken, the needy, the downtrodden. He knew their struggle, largely because it mirrored his own. He was always stepping out to help them.

Until the day Barry died—of sepsis in March 2018—he lived on less than $1,000 of income and government assistance per month, yet I saw him give food away nearly every week. I saw him give the good news about Jesus away even more. When I introduced Barry to a man just released from prison, Barry gave him a bed in his apartment within five minutes. The mission fused our friendship. I'd studied farming; Barry could see the harvest. God used us together in ways I never could've imagined. But he also used Barry to change me.

Friendship as a Mirror

I inhaled one piece of cheese bread after another as I stood by the kitchen sink. My wife told me to grab a plate, sit down, and slow down. I had tunnel vision. A complex counseling situation was crushing me. I was responding the way I'd responded so many times before: with food.

Suddenly, it dawned on me just how similar Barry and I were. Where I grew up, you didn't deal with stress through drugs or alcohol. Those things weren't acceptable, but other sin was. I ran to pizza because no one raised me to run to dope. But make no mistake: my kitchen counter was Barry's corner. His bar was my pizza shop. My sin was more culturally acceptable, but it was no less lethal when I leaned on it rather than God.

The Spirit began using Barry to expose *my* sinfulness. At a heart level, he and I were no different. We had different mentors, knew different neighborhoods, and were taught different ways to cope. My life was a mountain of undeserved kindness. I was raised in church; generations of my family knew Jesus; my education was phenomenal; my upbringing was sheltered.

Not so for Barry. His upbringing was different in almost every way. Yet there I was, nursing the same sinful habits with more culturally acceptable nameplates. Replacing God brings judgment, regardless of whether we use carbs or cocaine.

A psychologist might call my misunderstanding of Barry the Fundamental Attribution Error. When other people fail, you point to their flawed character or harmful intentions. Their failure is a problem with who they are or an expression of their hostility toward me. When I fail, however, I point to the circumstances and pressures in my life. *You're late because you're lazy or don't care. I'm late because I'm busy and it's been a crazy week.*

My pride told me that Barry was naïve and too soft on people, that his struggles were personal discipline problems. That man Barry housed straight out of prison? He stole Barry's coat. Those people who needed food? They could somehow afford cigarettes. My clinical analysis saw through them. In fact, I saw only the worst in them.

Other Side of the Tracks

Barry would often gently remind me: "You gotta remember, Wavey Gravey (his nickname for me), God gave you loving parents and a safe home and so many blessings. Lots of people are just trying to survive. They've almost never felt safe and they've never been taught."

I can't remember those words without tearing up. He was correct. I grew up on the "right" side of the tracks. I had—and still have—so much to learn. Barry wanted me to treat others in light of the grace God had shown me. The Spirit had created a gentle, merciful heart in that mountain of a man. Without Christ, Barry embraced the harsh facade a drug dealer wears to survive the street. God mercifully stripped Barry of that and replaced it with a Spirit-wrought gentleness toward the least, the last, and the lost. And he used Barry to strip away the pride in me.

The Spirit used Barry's understanding of the gospel to transform my perspective of myself. In Christ, we can both see sin clearly and also show mercy gently. Every person is a complex combination of villain and victim. They have done horrible things. Horrible things have been done to them. They need to turn from sin to Jesus Christ.

Every month I helped Barry with his budget. I did this for 11 years. And every month for 11 years I would bust him for spending more than he had on stupid stuff. But as I sat with a young man in seminary this morning, I told him, "You know what, Barry never got that stinkin' budget in order. Despite all that time I spent harassing him about it, he never got it down. But what does it matter now? Barry is with Jesus! He's experiencing unending joy in the presence of our King. Jesus didn't stiff-arm Barry at the door because his budget was out of whack—he embraced him with the love bestowed upon a righteous son. I see it now! The God who began a good work in Barry completed that work (Phil. 1:6) without needing me to get him all spiffed up and squared away."

God's truth deserves obedience and demands declaration. But sometimes, people like me need to take a chill pill and walk gently with those who struggle. The Spirit's the barber, and he'll get everyone lined up right in the end.

These lessons have transformed how I've gone about planting our church. You can't plant a church without gentleness (okay, you can, but you certainly won't lead it well). Gentleness is treating others in light of God's kindness toward you. A gentle man knows that God has produced the good in him—against his best efforts. A gentle man knows he's more sinful than others perceive. A gentle man understands the magnitude of God's mercy given him in Christ.

And this was Barry. Was he a messed-up sinner? You bet. But he knew it. And he reveled in the grace of God in Christ. Because of that, he was gentle. He's gone now, but I'm praying that God would make me more like my late, gentle friend.

34

3 WAYS TO AVOID BURNOUT

Kyllum Lewis

I know what you're thinking—another article about burnout. With so much already written on this topic, do we really need more? It seems we do. Despite the many helpful warnings, church planters continue to hit that wall. Whether a disastrous fall, or a gradual decline in spiritual vitality, burnout occurs in many different forms. We must continue broaching this pressing topic to save churches, marriages, families, and lives.

I know this all too well. In 2014 my soul was like that small chip on your car's front windshield. You know it's there, but it's not affecting your driving, so you ignore it. Only for me, while working toward our replant, that tiny crack began to spread rapidly into a shattered windshield. My mind, emotions, and body shut down. Severe anxiety attacks began to occur monthly, then weekly, then almost daily. Riddled with anxiety, I flamed out.

This doesn't have to be your story.

Church planting is a joyful yet arduous calling. Maintaining our joy is the tricky part. Three principles have helped my ongoing recovery; I hope they can help you avoid burnout while church planting.

1. Don't Formularize the Gospel

As our church plant sought to build a gospel culture, I turned issues "of first importance" (1 Cor. 15:3) into issues "of sole importance." Gospel-centrality became gospel-exclusivity. Christ and his salvation were the fix to every problem and the answer to every question. While it's true the gospel is what we *ultimately* need when planting a church, it's not the *only* thing we need. Developing leadership, communication, systems, and skills all play significant roles in establishing a healthy church.

In my immaturity, I also treated the gospel as law, because it told me what to do. In time, though, I realized the gospel is a beauty to behold, not a formula to use. We're to bathe in the ocean of Christ's grace, enjoying our union and ongoing communion with him (John 15). His Spirit gives rest to the weary, softens the hardhearted, cleanses the shame-filled, comforts the grieving, and restores the wounded soul.

Instead of formularizing the gospel, we should enjoy it.

2. Don't Neglect Soul Care

As a church planter, it's tempting to take on responsibility for many things—some of which aren't our responsibility—and neglect the very things for which we *are* responsible. Either way, the outcome is often a boosted ego or a crushed spirit.

Church planting includes embracing complex tensions involving time, energy, resources, and people. These tensions inevitably generate stress and bring disappointment, confusion, and hurt, all of which can seep into the crevasses of our hearts—hearts that God says we're responsible for (Prov. 4:23; 1 Tim. 4:16). As a young planter, I overlooked the importance of caring for my soul, and it cost me, my family, and our church.

We're better spouses, parents, friends, and leaders when we're physically, emotionally, and spiritually healthy. As we steward this responsibility, we'll be better equipped to care for those under our leadership. To "keep our hearts," we must establish healthy rhythms that place us on the front foot of prevention, not the back foot of recovery. Consider how to foster a rhythm of daily communion, weekly sabbath, monthly solitude, and yearly retreats. It'll be good for your soul.

3. Don't Ignore Wise Counsel

As we plant churches, we're going to experience great difficulties, carry heavy burdens, and even become wounded. It's critical that we build into our lives channels for wise counsel and oversight. We should surround ourselves with people who really see us—all our fears, anxieties, insecurities, frustrations, hurts, and sinful dispositions. People who can genuinely speak into our lives and assist us as we process pain, disappointment, forgiveness, and repentance.

One of the most significant changes I've made is to put in place what I call my three-piece band: my wife, one of our elders, and my counselor. They see and speak into my life, and have permission to communicate with each other when needed. For me, this has been incredibly freeing and healing.

We church planters are an energetic and ambitious bunch. But our zeal can often lead to burnout when we're trying to plant in our strength. As the apostle Paul wrote, "We proclaim him, admonishing and teaching everyone with all wisdom, so that we may present everyone perfect in Christ. To this end I also labor, striving with all his energy working powerfully within me" (Col. 1:28–29).

Like us, Paul worked hard for the kingdom of God. Yet he strove with energy not his own. This is a good reminder for weary church planters on the verge of burnout. The race we run is long, full of obstacles ready to steal our joy and crush our endurance. We need our Father to daily revive our souls and empower us to run our race well for his glory.

The gospel is for church planters, too.

35

WHY CHURCH PLANTING IS SO HARD

Jan Vezikov

Planting a church in Boston is the hardest thing I've ever done. It's cold. It's expensive. And people don't want us here. It's like we've started a business that offers a product everyone needs but no one wants.

The same is true for hard places all over the world.

You won't just be disliked and ignored; you'll be hated and opposed. Church planters, therefore, must be prepared to withstand opposition from three directions: outside, inside, and above the church.

Opposition from Outside

I knew planting in Boston would be hard. I was aware of the stats. But I wasn't prepared for how this opposition would affect virtually every aspect of life—from the struggle to reach sustainability to the seemingly impossible task of finding a space to rent for corporate worship.

And the direct opposition we've faced only makes these realities more difficult to endure. *So, you're planting a church? What kind? Open and affirming? You don't really believe Jesus is the only way to God, right? Surely you don't believe in hell?* But the "raised eyebrows" aren't so bad. What's taken getting used to is the outright hate. I'll never forget the letter I received a couple years into our church-planting journey.

"Jesus. Is. Evil."—written in bold letters across the top of the page. The anonymous author wasn't happy about our presence in the city. Here's a small taste of the letter's content, "If god exists, then god is evil; and, therefore, god does not deserve respect in any way, shape, or form. If this honest observation means I will be eternally punished, then at least I can rest assured that, as I burn, I will be in good company."

Initially, this letter haunted me. *How could someone be so against us? Why do we have to endure such opposition?* But then I was reminded of the words of Jesus: "If the world hates you, know that it has hated me before it hated you" (John 15:18).

I've come to take heart in the fact that this person knows we're in the city. I'll take hostility over indifference any day. And the opposition has given me fresh appreciation for Jesus's words in the Sermon on the Mount:

> Blessed are you when others revile you and persecute you and utter all kinds of evil against you falsely on my account. Rejoice and be glad, for your reward is great in heaven, for so they persecuted the prophets who were before you. (Matt. 5:11–12)

In the same sermon, Jesus said, "Love your enemies and pray for those who persecute you" (Matt. 5:44). I'm learning to receive the blessing of being reviled while praying fervently for those who oppose us.

Opposition from Inside

Opposition from outside the church stings; opposition from inside the church devastates. I'm used to having people storm out of worship services because the Scriptures offended them. I'm used to getting chewed out for holding to orthodox beliefs. But I don't think I'll ever get used to self-professing believers who sow discord among God's people.

The apostle Paul warned the Ephesian elders, "I know that after my departure fierce wolves will come in among you, not sparing the flock; and from among your own selves will arise men speaking twisted things, to draw away the disciples after them" (Acts 20:29–30). The most dangerous wolves don't look like wolves. They look like the sheep you've tended, fed, and loved. You see one sheep stray from the flock. Then another. You begin to notice a pattern. They were all part of the same community group, with the same leader. Someone you've loved and cared for has been drawing away disciples after them.

And most don't leave quietly. The emails usually begin, "Just a few parting words of advice . . ." Lately, much of the internal opposition has been about sexual ethics and/or gender issues. You better know the Scriptures and be prepared to defend the truth. No wonder Jesus warned, "Behold, I am sending you out as sheep in the midst of wolves, so be wise as serpents and innocent as doves" (Matt. 10:16).

The deepest wounds are often caused by those who were once members of your church. Perhaps your families were close, but they've decided to leave. You get an email like this: "While church planting is a good vision, it's not what we want in a church."

I've never been a super emotional guy. I'm Russian, and I was raised in New England. It's a miracle I can smile. But pastoring hurts. After you take a few of these emotional hits, it's tempting to harden your heart and withdraw. Don't. Hiding never brings healing. Only taking refuge in the Lord Jesus does. He was betrayed by those he loved, and you will be too. To plant a church, you need thick skin and a soft heart. Though this doesn't come naturally, we can look to Jesus, who is both fierce as a lion and tenderhearted as a lamb.

Opposition from Above

Before planting our church, I believed in the existence of Satan in theory. Now I know, without a shadow of a doubt, that Satan exists. Demons exist. They despise your church. They despise you. And they'll do everything they can to take you out. Be prepared for bouts of depression, spiritual funks, and heightened temptations. Be strong in the Lord and in the strength of his might (Eph. 6:10). He who is in you is greater than he who is in the world (1 John 4:4).

The god of this world has blinded the minds of

unbelievers, but Jesus opens blind eyes by the power of the Spirit (2 Cor. 4:4–6). So trust in him to build his church. The worst opposition, even the gates of hell, stands no chance against the advance of his church (Matt. 16:18)—no matter where you are or how hard it gets.

36

WHEN YOUR CHURCH ISN'T WHAT YOU DREAMED

Noel Heikkinen

Planting a church can be hazardous to your soul.

Obviously, there are more physically dangerous jobs on the planet, but when it comes to sheer spiritual danger, few occupations outrank "church planter." So before you quit your cushy job grinding asphalt, let me give you fair warning of what's to come.

Most people get into church planting for a few common reasons:

1. To see people far from Jesus put their faith in him.
2. To see their town, neighborhood, or city transformed by a vibrant community of faith.
3. To see a whole bunch of churches launch out of their new church.

These goals are Christ-exalting, thrilling, and, for most new churches, agonizingly slow to accomplish. That's why I wasn't surprised when I recently got this one-sentence email from a church planter: "I want to quit and need someone to talk me out of it."

This haunting sentence was penned by a passionate and godly man who had discovered the daily grind of church planting. Like countless planters before him, he learned the hard way that few people sprint through the doors of your new church, repenting of their sin and throwing themselves headlong into gospel ministry. Rather, the people you invite to church stare at you with incredulity when you tell them you meet in an elementary school gymnasium.

When a passionate church planter discovers the slow, difficult grind of church planting, secret idols are easily exposed. Even godly ambition can reveal hidden idols.

Steadfast Savior

The gospel you preach to weary people each week is the same gospel you desperately need. Let me remind you of what you already know: Jesus will never let you down (even when it feels like he has).

By every earthly indication, Jesus had let his disciples down. He told them he was leaving, and they were grappling with the reality of going it alone without him. He told them they would lose their spiritual family and get kicked out of the synagogue.

On top of all of that, Jesus lamented that there was a bunch of stuff he wished he could tell them, but couldn't. This was a new and terrifying reality, but he knew what they needed to hear: "Truly, truly, I say to you, you will weep and lament, but the world will rejoice. You will be sorrowful, but your sorrow will turn into joy" (John 16:20).

In hindsight, we know Jesus is talking about his death, burial, resurrection, and ascension. But there are echoes of his promise that reach into the churches the apostles were to plant—and to the churches we plant 2,000 years later.

It will be tough. You will have sorrow.

Sorrow is woven into the fabric of our world, and that includes church planting. It's not going to be an easy ride. Plans will fail. People will disappoint you. Your church may not—probably *will* not—be all you thought it would be. And this makes what Jesus said next all the more glorious: "So also you have sorrow now, but I will see you again, and your hearts will rejoice, and no one will take your joy from you" (John 16:22).

Your heart *will* rejoice. No one will take your joy from you. This is true for you, just as it was true for the disciples. You will see Jesus, and the immediate effect will be joy—true, lasting joy that cannot be taken away. In church planting, as in life generally, you have the strange capacity to feel joy and sorrow in the same minute. One minute you rejoice at someone coming to know Christ; in the next you have to make a difficult call in a pastoral situation.

If you tie your spiritual wellbeing to your circumstances, your life will be a never-ending emotional whirlwind. Don't do it.

Certain Hope

Jesus knows this to be true of us. He knows that life in this world—especially our efforts to make him known—will bring tribulation. We will experience hardship. But Jesus offers us a stable peace amid a troubling world: "I have said these things to you, that in me you may have peace. In the world you will have tribulation. But take heart; I have overcome the world" (John 16:33).

In Christ alone, there is peace. Peace through the storms that church planting will bring.

As you seek to plant churches that put the glory of Christ on display, tribulation will come. But don't lose heart: Christ has overcome the world. We plant churches to take *this* glorious message to the world. We long for more people to have joy and peace in Christ in this world full of tribulation.

So take heart, but also guard your heart. The task of church planting is glorious, but it is not ultimate. Like anything besides Christ, church planting makes for a bad savior.

If planting your church begins to mean more to you than Jesus does, the slow grind will become a slow death. When you forget that Jesus will never let you down, empty chairs on a gymnasium floor can accuse your soul and breed bitterness in your heart.

But when you lift your eyes to Jesus, who sits at the right hand of God the Father, you can remember that you are loved. He has not abandoned you. And he will never fail you.

SECTION THREE | MISSION

Mission

: a specific task with which a person or a group is charged

: calling, vocation

: to send on or entrust with a mission

– Merriam-Webster's Unabridged Dictionary

Then Jesus came to them and said, "All authority in heaven and on earth has been given to me. Therefore go and make disciples of all nations, baptizing them in the name of the Father and of the Son and of the Holy Spirit, and teaching them to obey everything I have commanded you. And surely I am with you always, to the very end of the age."

– Matthew 28:18–20

The grand arch of the Bible story reveals a holy and merciful God creating for himself a people, blessing them, and calling them to extend his blessing to the nations. One day all tongues and tribes will gather before Christ's throne . . . until then, the church is God's mission strategy. *We* are his means of scattering light in darkness. In Christ, we are the light!

As we delight in Jesus—loving one another, obeying him, proclaiming the gospel—the world sees God's kingdom in action. This is the church's call, the continuing mission of Jesus, and the heartbeat of Acts 29.

37

HOW CAN YOU TELL IF A CHURCH IS GOSPEL-CENTERED? START WITH THE PULPIT.

Yancey Arrington

The tagline "gospel-centered" has become commonplace in the church-planting world. In many ways, this is a good thing.

But we do well to ask: *What exactly does the phrase mean? Does the planter have to be committed to mention Jesus in every sermon? Must there be a mandatory invitation to salvation in each service?*

One of the best ways to "test" gospel-centrality in the life of a church plant is to look at the pulpit. A church may have "gospel-centered" peppered throughout their statement of beliefs and on their website, but one of clearest places to see whether gospel-centrality is a real value—or simply a buzzword—is when the pastor preaches God's Word on Sunday.

The King Has Won

Before looking at the specifics of gospel-centered preaching, consider the following illustration.[34]

Imagine a king departing his castle to battle an invading army. If the king loses, he sends his military advisers

[34] For more on this, see Tim Keller's message, "What Is Gospel-Centered Ministry?" *The Gospel Coalition*, May 28, 2007: https://www.thegospelcoalition.org/conference_media/gospel-centered-ministry/ accessed on Jan. 18, 2021.

back to the castle with the bad news. They also inform the citizens of new strategies and techniques: "The enemy is approaching. We suggest you put marksmen here, chariots there, and so on." All of this is done in an attempt to equip the people to defeat the enemy themselves. They feel incredible pressure, knowing that victory (or defeat) rests on their shoulders.

But if the king defeats the enemy, he sends his messengers back with the *good* news. They return to the castle square shouting: "The king has defeated the enemy! Enjoy the peace and blessings of the victory our lord has achieved for you!" With this joyous declaration, the people would not only experience freedom in their daily lives, but their love and gratitude would also be directed toward their king.

What is a gospel-centered church? In a manner of speaking, a gospel-centered church labors to stress—in her messages, ministries, and mission—that, in Christ's finished work on the cross, God has achieved victory. The King has truly won.

"Good Advice" Preaching

How does this approach affect preaching? Painting broadly, the typical contemporary church often markets the preaching as "relevant" and "practical." Many will have something like the following on their websites: "Come see how what we say will meet your everyday needs with biblical principles that show God's Word is true." Further, many church planters are told (by church-growth "experts") that this is the best way to gather a crowd large enough to gain sufficient momentum to get their fledging plants off the ground.

Consequently, congregants can be given an imbalanced rotation of topical sermons on money, family, marriage, and the like. Often the primary aim of such messages isn't so much to exalt Christ and his cross work as it is to focus on practical applications. In short, what people can get is not the gospel, but a bunch of "good" advice.

In essence, much of the application sounds barely

different from what you'd find in the latest self-help books or talk-shows. The hope is that hearers leave with sermon notes packed with practical "to-dos" to employ at home, work, school, and in other spheres of life. This doesn't mean these kinds of sermons never use the Bible or even talk about Jesus. On the contrary, it's not uncommon to see "good advice" preachers insert Jesus at the conclusion of their sermons. They may even emphasize the fact that Christ wants to save people, and that they can receive salvation by saying a prayer, coming down an aisle, filling out a card, and so on.

Again, this kind of preaching strategy may seem effective for a young church plant. Attenders will likely compliment pastors on how insightful and practical they are. After all, sermon content has been focused squarely on their worlds of concern. They want "success" in life, and any tips to achieve that success are welcome.

The potential problems with such preaching are numerous. But at its core, good-advice preaching makes the Bible about us instead of God. Jesus is relegated to being *part* of Scripture's story, instead of the sum and substance of it all.

Consequently, this kind of preaching leads listeners to think that while salvation is about Jesus, the rest of their spiritual growth is, for all practical purposes, up to them. Therefore good-advice preaching, no matter how well-meaning, is actually untethered from the gospel because it grounds people in law, not grace.

This is problematic, for the true gospel insists that Jesus's person and work not only enables my growth, but also empowers and sustains it. The gospel is not just a doorway we walk through into the Christian life, but the very room we live in. This ought to be the refrain of gospel-centered sermons: that Christian growth rests upon—and is enabled by—Christ's finished work and the Spirit's faithful power.

Paul's Preaching

What might Paul say about "good advice" preaching? "I decided to know nothing among you except Jesus Christ and him crucified" (1 Cor. 2:2). Paul frames his ministry—including his preaching—as being centered on Jesus. And not just any perspective on Jesus—he homes in on his work on the cross.

In other words, Paul preached on various "real-life" topics, but he did so in such a way that Jesus wasn't seen as just another (albeit better) life coach, self-help expert, Mr. Fix It, or success guru. In Paul's preaching, Jesus is the crucified and risen Lord. There is no other option, because there is no other Jesus.

Similarly, it's not that gospel-centered churches don't talk about what followers of Jesus should do in the various circles of daily life. It's just that they intentionally tie the doing to the being. That is, all our doing in the Christian life flows from the definitive "done" that was Christ's work on the cross (John 19:30).

Thus, gospel-centered church plants have preaching in which the good news of the gospel not only shapes the sermon's conclusion, but its body as well. We are, after all, more proclaimers than advisers.

The world doesn't need more people who (merely) give good advice. The world needs churches fluent in the gospel, characterized by preaching that centers on Jesus Christ and him crucified. This is preaching where the congregants' "dos" rest upon Christ's "done."

38

THE SECRET TO CHURCH PLANTING (FROM A FORMER MUSLIM)

Adam Muhtaseb

As a former Muslim, the questions still sound strange. *Is this passage too intense for visitors? Does my sermon have enough jokes? Should we do an iPad giveaway?* These questions ran through my mind as we launched Redemption City Church in Baltimore. Indeed, such thoughts can haunt any new church planter as we try to determine what will win people's hearts and get them to stay.

Much of today's church-planting strategy promotes a "bait and switch" approach. Bring out the bells and whistles to attract the masses. Then, once people come—once they're comfortable—switch things up by sneaking in more nibbles of the gospel.

This temptation to bait and switch unbelievers is so different from what I saw growing up in a Muslim family. In a mosque, there's no fancy stage, no Hillsong United Muslim songs, no mood lighting. The world's fastest growing religion doesn't try to lure people with entertainment.[35] They believe Allah and the Quran's message are compelling enough. Muslims win people to their faith through their message. A 1,500-year-old message from a still-dead prophet seems to be enough. Islam offers

---

[35] Michael Lipka and Conrad Hackett, "Why Muslims are the World's Fastest Growing Religious Group," *Pew Research Center*, April 6, 2017: https://www.pewresearch.org/fact-tank/2017/04/06/why-muslims-are-the-worlds-fastest-growing-religious-group/ accessed on Jan. 18, 2021.

a religious to-do list that *might* help you avoid the fires of hell if you live a good enough life. That's their message, and it scared me enough to keep going.

But what brought me to Jesus wasn't fear or a church's bells and whistles. It was a better message. It was the gospel. When Islam choked me with "Do, do, do," Jesus said, "It's already done" and captured my heart. That's how a Muslim kid eventually became a Christian church planter in one of America's most unreached cities.

Gospel Gives What We Need

Now if Islam is the fastest-growing religion in the world, and Christ's church has an exponentially better message than Islam, why are we still trying to win people to Jesus with props?

Some churches' philosophy is, "Give the people what they want." Henry Ford, founder of Ford Motor Company, once said, "If I had asked customers what they wanted, they would have told me, 'A faster horse.'" If Ford focused on the market research, he never would have built a car.

Often, planters and pastors focus exclusively on "market research." They cater to what lost people seem to want instead of what they actually need. The problem is, people don't truly perceive what they need (Rom. 3:10–17), and you'll never be able to give them what they want as well as the world can.

Gospel Captures Hearts

The gospel tells the exhausted college graduate that his value doesn't come from his career, but from Jesus's finished work. It tells the single woman that Jesus provides the comfort and security she longs for. It tells the son grieving his father's death that Jesus turns the end into an eternal beginning.

No matter the individual. No matter the context. No matter the city. The gospel is what gets people to come, and it gets them to stay. Will some people come and leave because you didn't scratch their itch? Absolutely. If you faithfully preach the truth, however, over time the gospel will capture more and more hearts.

Even in an unchurched, post-Christian city like Baltimore, you don't need bells and whistles. It's ok if your hospitality team is a work in progress. You can have just one guy in the band. None of that matters because you already have the one thing you really need—the too-good-to-be-true news of complete acceptance by God through Jesus.

Gospel Must Be Preached

Remember Paul's final counsel to Timothy, his protégé church planter? "Preach the word; be ready in season and out of season" (2 Tim. 4:2). Through the trials of church planting, our job is to preach the Scriptures. This is our age-old strategy to both reach people and keep people.

If we choose to emphasize anything other than proclaiming the gospel, sure, we may attract people with our flash and sizzle. But what we *win* people with is what we'll have to *keep* them with. If we win people with the beauty of the gospel, the gospel will keep them.

Don't buy the lie that people aren't interested in the gospel. When unchurched people come to Redemption City, they're expecting to hear the Bible. I'd never go to a mosque, sit down, hear the imam teach, and think, *He's teaching from the Quran? Didn't expect that.* Lost visitors don't mind hearing the Bible from us; they expect to. So preach to fill others' hearts with so much love for Jesus that it pushes out love for sin, self, and the world.

After just two years of church planting, I've seen the gospel not only reach people, but keep them. Our church hasn't gone from five to 500 overnight. Yet it has grown steadily. We're closer to financial self-sustainability and multiplication simply from faithfully proclaiming the gospel in a culturally relevant and engaging way and addressing people's deepest needs with life's greatest news.

The gospel still works. Church planters, let's believe this with all our hearts. It's the power of God for salvation to everyone who believes (Rom. 1:16). May this conviction shape our ministries, sermons, vision, and mission.

39

DON'T OVERCOMPLICATE EVANGELISM

Tony Merida

"If you build it, they will come."

I like the movie *Field of Dreams*, but it's a terrible evangelism strategy for church planters.

Most unbelievers have no interest in joining you this Sunday. Simply offering a "good product" isn't enough in this post-Christian world. It doesn't matter how cool your venue is, how good your music and coffee are, or how hip your pastor looks.

The unbelievers who do show up are there because someone has befriended and invited them *outside* the walls of a church building. Most outsiders aren't waking up saying, "I wonder if they have good coffee. I'm going to check it out." Or "I bet the music is great there. I should go visit."

As church-planting pastors, we have to overemphasize evangelism. It's a challenge for us to be both missional and also pastoral—a tension that exists from the founding of your church. One planter recently told me, "I just got started, and I already have shepherding issues."

But if a church is to flourish, evangelism must be central to the life of the body.

Models of Evangelism

In years past, two forms of evangelism have been most common: *event* evangelism and *cold-call* evangelism. Indeed, when people hear "evangelism" today, they often think of either big events/crusades or door-to-door outreach.

The Lord has used both of these approaches, and in some contexts, they continue to be effective. However, in other places—particularly in many post-Christian contexts—these approaches are often less fruitful.

I don't want to insinuate we should reject these approaches. We shouldn't. But I want to highlight another approach that has historic precedent—one that is both culturally appropriate and personally achievable: *network evangelism.*

Network evangelism isn't an event; it's not a program; it's not something you only do on Tuesday nights at 6 p.m. It's a lifestyle. It's about living with gospel intentionality in the everyday rhythms of life. It's done among the people who fall into your current web of relationships.

When planting a church, network evangelism becomes a practical way to emphasize how every member can live as a missionary. In order to cultivate and sustain an evangelistic culture in our young church, I've preached a number of sermons on this topic. The first series came after the elders had a long discussion about why we weren't seeing more people converted. As I was praying and thinking about how to lead our people, I came across this statement in Tim Keller's *Church Planter Manual*:

> There must be an atmosphere of expectation that every member will always have two to four people in the incubator, a force-field in which people are being prayed for, given literature, brought to church or other events.[36]

We've sought to expand and build on this idea.

Why Network Evangelism?

Network evangelism first recognizes the sovereignty of God. It develops a mindset that every person in our sphere of life matters, and it helps us remember that God has us

[36] Timothy J. Keller and J. Allen Thompson, *Redeemer Church Planting Manual* (Redeemer City to City, 2002).

living in this time and place in history, surrounded by particular image-bearers he has sovereignly put in our path (Acts 17:26).

Additionally, network evangelism has historic precedent. In his book *Cities of God*, sociologist Rodney Stark describes how Christianity became an urban movement that transformed the Roman world:

> Social networks are the basic mechanism through which conversion takes place. . . . Most conversions are not produced by professional missionaries conveying a new message, but by rank-and-file members who share their faith with their friends and relatives. . . . The principle that conversions spread through social networks is quite consistent with the fact that the earliest followers of Jesus shared many family ties and long-standing associations. . . . Although the very first Christian converts in the West may have been by full-time missionaries, the conversion process soon became self-sustaining as new converts accepted the obligation to spread their faith and did so by missionizing their immediate circle of intimates.[37]

Did you see that? The movement advanced because new converts accepted the obligation to spread the gospel within their own circles of everyday influence.

Further, network evangelism promotes faithfulness and patience. Evangelistic methods often involve only "on the spot" presentations. They can be impersonal as well. They can be about generating numbers, not valuing people. They can allow us to simply "check a box" to appease our guilt, and then move on.

But when you're reaching out to people you see regularly, it demands faithfulness and perseverance. You can do the necessary pre-evangelism, answer questions, slowly and gradually watch defenses go down, and hopefully—by God's grace—see your friend, family member, coworker, or neighbor declare, "Jesus is Lord."

---

[37] Rodney Stark, *Cities of God: The Real Story of How Christianity Became an Urban Movement and Conquered Rome* (HarperCollins Publishers, 2007), 13–14.

Who's in Your Networks?

We could organize our web of relationships in a variety of ways, but it has been helpful for our church to think within five categories:

1. **Familial Network:** people in your family.
2. **Geographical Network:** people in your neighborhood.
3. **Vocational Network:** people at your workplace.
4. **Recreational Network:** people you hang out with.
5. **Commercial Network:** people you see at shops.

We encouraged our church members to identify at least five people in each of these networks—or if they're low in one area, to increase the number of people in the other networks. And we've encouraged them to do one of five tasks:

1. **Pray for them**: You'll be surprised what happens when you begin to pray for the people in your path. You may experience the joy C. S. Lewis expressed: "I have two lists of names in my prayers, those for whose conversions I pray and those for whose conversions I give thanks. The little trickle of transferences from List A to List B is a great comfort."
2. **Invite them:** Invite them over to eat dinner, to play sports, to go to a movie, to come with you to a church event.
3. **Serve them:** Identify a way that you can bless those in your networks. Babysit for them, pick up groceries for them, cut their grass, and so on.
4. **Give resources to them:** Ask them to read a book or article with you, or to listen to a sermon or podcast. Discuss these resources with them.
5. **Share the gospel with them:** Look for various places where you can talk about your faith. Let your friend know you are part of a church and see if they ask questions. Listen to their problems with real concern, and then seize the opportunity to address the problems with gospel hope. Share

some of your own struggles and talk about how you deal with them in light of your faith. Simply ask them what they believe, and just let them talk.

From this plan—five people in each of the five categories, doing one of the five tasks—we developed this evangelism card for individuals and small groups:

Network Evangelism *Pray. Invite. Give Literature. Serve. Share the gospel.*	
Networks	**People**
Vocational	
Familial	
Geographical	
Commercial	
Recreational/Relational	

May God use ordinary saints like us, who overflow with love for the Savior, to lead outsiders to faith as we live with gospel intentionality in our everyday networks.

40

PASTOR, YOUR SHEEP ARE NOT AN ACCIDENT

Tyler St. Clair

Maybe it's just me, but holidays like Christmas and Easter are always weird and complicated in ministry. I become preoccupied with who's there, who's not, and what everyone is thinking. *Will the music be to their liking? Will I preach in a way that is accessible yet bold? Will these people come back?* and so on . . .

Unfortunately, this past Easter was no different. Despite our service being well attended and going surprisingly well, I still wrestled with a lack of contentment the following week. After God convicted me and I repented, I was reminded of a simple—yet all too easy to forget—truth: I'm called to pastor those whom God has put in front of me.

Worldly Idealism

It's easy for church planters to dream of the kind of church they'd like to plant and lead. After all, we need to envision what the church we plan to start will look like, and part of that involves thinking about the people we need to make those plans happen. In many ways, this process is normal in seeing a healthy church planted and established.

And yet there are inherent dangers in this process. In our sin, it's easy to operate from a worldly idealism, which inevitably leads to growing frustrated with what God has given us now. Whether it's the slow rate of growth, a lack of leaders, a financial shortfall, or something else, discontentment can subtly seep into a church planter's heart. And when we're discontent with the church God has given us, we won't be able to obey Peter's command to "shepherd the flock of God among you" (1 Pet. 5:2).

Church planter, how often do you look to seemingly greener pastoral pastures? Do you peer over the fence and envy another's flock? I've been guilty of this myself. Here are three particular dangers to this kind of discontentment.

1. Pragmatism

When we're not satisfied with the church God has given us to shepherd, pragmatism is a possible pitfall. *Just add water and stir, and you'll get these amazing results*, pragmatism whispers. I've seen it many times; well-meaning church planters resort to the latest gimmicks, fads, and methods—often doing a kind of copy and paste from another "successful" ministry. There's nothing wrong with learning from others, but this must never replace faithfulness to the task at hand.

Overly pragmatic planters exchange the shepherd's rod and staff for "what's new" or the latest formula for success. And when such methods, rather than the Bible, become our functional authority, we're in more trouble than meets the eye. Further, one subtle danger of pragmatism in church planting is that you may gather people, but you may not disciple or shepherd them.

2. Overlook

It's difficult to love your people well if you're constantly focusing on who's not there. Of course, we should be evangelistic—I'm not suggesting we abandon a fervent desire to reach the lost. But we mustn't overlook our flock in our zeal to reach more people.

Our people need us focused on discipleship, leading the church well by the Spirit's power. They need us to labor as we prepare to preach God's Word; they need us to be fervent in prayer; and they need us to lead them to the

Good Shepherd, time and again. We do all of this with the flock God has given us, not the "church of our dreams."

Church planters won't be in tune with their peoples' needs if they're constantly looking past them to the horizon of what lies ahead.

3. Miss God's grace

Further, if you're always living in the future, not only will you miss what God has graciously done in the past, you're likely to look past the work he's currently doing.

During Israel's transition from slaves in Egypt to possessors of the promised land, the Lord repeatedly commanded that they remember and recall his deliverance and mighty deeds (Deut. 6; 8). But they consistently rebelled by turning to idols. And we're no different. When we fail to see God's grace, given to us daily, we wander, and our hearts are drawn to other things.

Shepherd from Among the Flock

One reason I love my wife significantly more than the waitress who routinely takes my order at the neighborhood Coney Island (my favorite greasy-spoon restaurant here in Detroit) is proximity. While my favorite waitress knows my order and is kind, my wife knows me intimately and we share deep love. More than that, I've made a covenant with my wife (something I haven't done with the Coney Island waitress).

As planters, it is of chief importance that we love the people God has put under our spiritual care. We have covenanted with them, and they are the sheep with whom we have closest relations. We cannot merely pastor people from the pulpit (as important as that is). We must also minister to them in their living rooms and on their front porches.

I can personally attest to how proximity with the flock God has given me has softened my heart toward them. The more I'm with the sheep, the more I love them, and the more vibrant my prayer life is concerning them. At the same time, proximity reveals my sin. This can be painful, but by God's grace it has driven me to deeper dependence on the Lord Jesus. Walking closely with the flock also clarifies pastoral needs in the midst of both the mundane and mania of church planting. Yes, reaching more people is important, but so is caring for the flock God has given you.

To love people well, we must be proactive in prayer and persistent in our pursuit of wandering sheep. Robust and implemented church membership, encouraged accountability among the church family, much prayer, and intentional shepherding have allowed us to see many wanderers return home.

Church planter, your primary task is to shepherd the sheep God has given you. Do this by taking them to the Good Shepherd, over and over.

41

HOW FORCED WITHDRAWAL MIGHT FURTHER THE MISSION

Adam Ramsey

So much has changed. And rapidly. Most of us have been required to make unprecedented adjustments in our work, travel, worship, finances, and social arrangements. With COVID-19's march across the globe, the unified call has been to temporarily withdraw from the lives to which we're all accustomed.

It was only a few years ago that Rod Dreher's *The Benedict Option* caused a splash in the Western church by calling for a strategic withdrawal to rebuild a deep, devoted counterculture within the church that would be able to weather the growing storm of secular hostility. Dreher's argument was that we should "stop trying to meet the world on its own terms and focus on building up fidelity in distinct community."[38] In this way, a backward step that gains formational distance in the lives of God's people might serve as the missional equivalent of Muhammad Ali's *rope-a-dope*—a tactic used to conserve energy for the long haul when needing to outlast an aggressive and unrelenting opponent.

During COVID-19, Western society has shifted almost overnight from an emphasis on individualism (live as you please and be true to yourself) to collectivism (follow these rules and do your part for society). Though certainly not

---

[38] Rod Dreher, *The Benedict Option: A Strategy for Christians in a Post-Christian Nation* (Penguin Random House, 2017), 121.

the kind of withdrawal church planters would've ever asked for, I wonder how this forced withdrawal from our comforts and rhythms—and from one another—might be strategically stewarded?

Could it be that this time of distancing has accomplished for us the necessary strategic withdrawal that many of us were hesitant to take? Could it be that the very real pressure and stretching we are all experiencing is merely the Divine Hand drawing the slingshot back, in order to propel us further into his redemptive plan than any of us could have ever strategized or imagined? We don't know how long this season will last or how painful it will be. But like all other trials, let's make sure we don't waste it. Here's three ways church planters can steward it well.

1. Gain Perspective

There are times when a backward step is necessary to disrupt unhealthy practices and regain perspective for the next move forward. As Mark Sayers points out in one of his excellent books, such distance from the prevailing culture "allows us to recognize the cultural myths and blind spots" we have bought into, perhaps more than we ever realized before.[39]

What if we used some of this extra space to reevaluate the integrity of our discipleship and the kind of fruit our approach to mission has been producing? What if we committed with new energy to creating rhythms and communities in our church plants that are sustainable not only in seasons of predictability and prosperity, but also in seasons of scarcity and uncertainty?

2. Go Deep

Perhaps the Benedict Option has come to us in the most unexpected of ways, but it nonetheless presents church planters with a magnificent opportunity. We now have to examine ourselves and hit reset on some of the ways we approach making disciples, strengthening families, and living on mission.

---

[39] Mark Sayers, *Disappearing Church: From Cultural Relevance to Gospel Resilience* (Moody Publishers, 2016), 153.

With new space comes opportunity for new depth. What if we trained our people to spend this time in such a way that we emerged from it with unprecedented biblical literacy? What if our increased solitude was used for increased intimacy in prayer and dependence on the Holy Spirit? What if this change of pace was a gift to us church planters and pastors, slowing us down in the right ways to deepen our patience and increase our ministry longevity?

3. Prepare for Re-entry

Colin Marshall and Tony Payne concluded their 2009 discipleship book, *The Trellis and the Vine*, with hauntingly prophetic words:

> Imagine that [a] pandemic swept through your part of the world, and that all public assemblies of more than three people were banned by the government for reasons of public health and safety. And let's say that due to some catastrophic combination of local circumstances, this ban had to remain in place for 18 months . . . there would be no services to run . . . no group activities or events of any kind to organize, administer, drum up support for, or attend. Just personal teaching and discipling and training your people in turn to be disciple makers. Here's the interesting question: after 18 months, when the ban was lifted and you were able to recommence Sunday gatherings and all the rest of the meetings of church life, what would you do differently?[40]

At some point, this crisis is going to end. The question for all of us is, *Do we really want to go back to the way things were?* Perhaps during this season, God is giving church-planting pastors an opportunity to examine the previous ways in which we allocated energy and resources—and whether we were prioritizing the right things.

Our plans may have changed for the moment, but that

---

[40] Colin Marshall and Tony Payne, *The Trellis and the Vine: The Ministry Mind-Shift That Changes Everything* (Matthias Media, 2009), 165–67.

may be one of the best things to happen to us, to bring us in step with God's plan, which has not changed. Wouldn't it be like God to bring the greatest renewal the church of this generation has ever seen through the greatest trial we have ever faced? May God use this crisis to bring us to the end of ourselves. And there, in the place of confessed weakness, meet us with revitalizing power.

42

HOW AN INTERNATIONAL PARTNERSHIP COULD BENEFIT YOUR CHURCH

Jen Oshman

Your weeks are crazy. There's the worship-team meeting, weekly small group, counseling that couple in crisis—oh, and a sermon to write. Add to that your worship space was unexpectedly pulled out from under you, and your children's ministry director just stepped down.

I can relate. My husband and I have served as church planters in both the United States and also abroad for nearly two decades. We know how easily the tyranny of the urgent rules a church planter's days. Often it's a great joy. Sometimes it's a painful slog. But always, we fall into bed exhausted. Church planting is hard work.

And so, it's as unintended as it is certain—urgent, daily needs in ministry are strong gravity, pulling us farther and farther away from where we meant to go with our church plants.

Inevitable Inward Drift

Church planters are by definition missional. We're passionate about making disciples; otherwise we wouldn't be out here.

But the great care required by our local churches leaves us with little energy for the *going to the nations* part of the Great Commission. Our local needs cause us to drift inward, inevitably pushing out our good intentions for global kingdom work.

Additionally, there's confusion and intimidation. To avoid making a global mess, we'd rather stick to what we know in our own neighborhoods. Or we wait for the elusive day when we have the budget, staff, or size that we think is needed for a global partnership.

As a result, we ensure the growth of our churches, but forsake the global mission. But it doesn't have to be this way. Growing an international church-planting partnership is not as hard as it seems, and—surprisingly—it may just be the best way to disciple our own communities along the way.

Global Growth Begets Local Growth

Counter to culture, our flesh, and church-growth programs, real discipleship takes place not when we cater to ourselves, but when we sacrifice ourselves on behalf of others. The abundant life (John 10:10) is found when we lay ourselves down for others, for the sake of Jesus's name (Matt. 16:25).

Insofar as our churches join in the discipleship of other nations, our church members will also be discipled. Jesus poured himself out that we might go and do likewise. This—*this!*—is the joy-filled, upside-down, counterintuitive way to pursue Christlikeness. It will take time. Years are needed to cross geographic, linguistic, cultural, and traditional barriers. Those who've experienced success say it takes at least three years of intentionality to see real fruit in both church bodies. But it's worth it.

God *will be* exalted among the nations (Ps. 46:10), and though it requires some temporary effort, it's for our eternal joy. God is already building his church overseas. He doesn't need us. But he does invite us.

Mutually Beneficial

A cross-cultural partnership gives two different people groups exposure to the diverse expressions of their one shared faith. It is rich and stretching for all involved. A mutually beneficial relationship blossoms through communication, time spent together, praying for one another, and bearing one another's financial burdens.

When possible, church leaders and teams should visit one another. Each visitor is an ambassador, carrying stories, photos, and needs back and forth. Eventually, the well-worn path between the two communities will grow cross-cultural friendships not unlike the early church, where "all who believed were together and had all things in common" (Acts 2:44).

We Western Christians are accustomed to taking short-term mission trips, feeling a sense of awe and accomplishment, and then returning home. Our partners overseas tell us this is unhelpful and usually harmful. Yet they insist that short-term trips can be effective—when the long-term health of the receiving community is in view. With every visit and team we send, we must ask our hosts, "How can we increase the strength of your local body? How can we enhance what you're already doing?" In humility, we must set aside preconceived notions, listen, and adjust.

There is much we can learn from our partners who experience different obstacles than we do. For example, in Europe there are far fewer Christians, or in some Asian nations less freedom, or in some African countries fewer material resources. To visit is to learn, observe, encourage, and offer help that is specific and requested.

Between visits churches can post one another's photos, send out updates and prayer needs, or plan ahead for holidays with cards. Each context will dictate what's appropriate, and each church should be open about what is beneficial, but they should view one another as extended family.

Last, and most anxiety-inducing, finances play a role. Globally wealthy churches should give sacrificially, but with the careful direction of the receiving church. It's vital that the relationship not be paternalistic, but rooted in brotherhood. This can be achieved through transparency, humility, and the assistance of other churches who have done this well before.

Next Steps

The Holy Spirit promises to empower us as we bear

witness to Jesus in our Judea, Samaria, and to the ends of the earth (Acts 1:8). Our God will be faithful as we seek to correct our churches' inward drift.

Visit Acts29.com (or your church-planting network's website) to see where churches are being planted. Contact area leaders for help and to ask questions. See who might be interested in starting a partnership.

At home, we must pray with our ministry leaders and congregations about shifting from an inward focus to an outward passion for God's global renown. May the Holy Spirit ignite a fire among us for giving, praying, and going to the nations.

We know that at the name of Jesus *every* knee will bow and *every* tongue confess (Phil. 2:10–11). Let's not forsake the eternal and global, then, for the urgent and local. As we seek to glorify God around the world, let's watch him grow our local churches too.

43

5 WAYS TO TEACH KIDS TO LOVE CHURCH PLANTING

Christy Britton

My husband and I are raising four boys. One of the things they know, without a shadow of a doubt, is that on Saturdays in the fall we gather with friends to watch the LSU Tigers play football. Our home fills with fans dressed in purple and gold. We visit, eat, and look after the little ones all while rooting for our favorite team.

Cheering for LSU is part of our family culture. We're proud to be well on our way to raising the next generation of LSU football fans.

But what else are we raising them to be? What does the culture of our home esteem to be of eternal significance?

My husband and I have been greatly influenced by our local church's commitment to planting churches—in both the United States and beyond. And we want our family to be about making disciples of all nations, which is accomplished best through the local church. Therefore, we're raising our boys in a church-planting culture.

"Extended" Family

Our kids are familiar with each of the church planters sent out from our local church. They are like extended family. We pray for and give to them. We talk about the necessity of church planting and challenge our kids to participate in this vital mission when they grow up.

We want our kids to view their participation in church planting as normal. We don't want them to grow up thinking about church planters in terms of "us" and "them." Since we want them to identify with the work and participate in it in various ways, we're raising them in an environment where church planting is an everyday aspect of a gospel-shaped lifestyle. It's what "we" do.

How, then, do we normalize church planting for our kids? Consider five suggestions.

1. Establish a church-planting culture in your home

There are several good ways to do this. First, surround your family with church planting by covenanting with a church committed to this endeavor. You may consider being part of a church plant yourselves (after all, a church-planting team requires more than just the pastor).

You can financially support church plants, and make sure your kids know other church planters. One way to do this is by keeping pictures and prayer cards of church planters on your fridge. Read church planters' newsletters aloud at the dinner table, then pray for them and their ministries. Visit church planters and offer to host them when they come to town.

2. Eliminate inconsistencies in your words and actions

Kids aren't stupid. If there are inconsistencies between what we say and what we do, they're likely to sniff them out. Parents, you won't get away with talking up disciple-making among the nations without some skin in the game. Encourage your kids toward the church-planting lifestyle by embracing it yourselves. If you say you're passionate about planting churches, then be about the business of planting churches. Kids learn best by seeing something in action and emulating it. Allow your kids to both hear and also see your passion.

3. Endeavor to connect their work to God's work

Disciples make disciples. If your children are united with Christ, then the Great Commission is for them. Train them to long for the glory of God and the eternal good of others. Show them how various professions can further the cause of church planting. After all, to see healthy churches planted, we need more than just pastors: We need mechanics, teachers, and stay-at-home moms. We need business owners, real-estate agents, and students. As the apostle Paul writes,

> Whatever you do, work heartily, as for the Lord and not for men, knowing that from the Lord you will receive the inheritance as your reward. You are serving the Lord Christ. (Col. 3:23–24)

Aim to teach your kids to connect their vocation to this mission.

4. Expect them to take part in church planting

Think about your expectations for your children. Many of us expect our kids to make good grades, get into good schools, be good citizens, and take care of us when we're older. These are all good things. But do we expect them to participate in church planting?

Teach them to love the church and the lost, then show them how both of these loves meet in church planting. Help your sons and daughters envision themselves as part of a church-planting team.

5. Encourage their hearts in the Lord

Your children have an Enemy who hates them. As they pursue the ministry of reconciliation, he will pursue their destruction. Encourage them. Remind them of the great promises of God. Pray with and for them.

And keep before them a vision of that "great multitude that no one could number, from every nation, from all tribes and peoples and languages, standing before the throne and before the Lamb, clothed in white robes, with palm branches in their hands, and crying out with a loud voice, 'Salvation belongs to our God who sits on the throne, and to the Lamb!'" (Rev. 7:9–10). Entice them with the glory of what's to come.

Future Church Planters

We spend a lot of energy encouraging our kids to chase their dreams. Are we encouraging them to pursue Christ and his kingdom by planting churches? Are we raising kids who will obey the Great Commission? Parents, cultivate your child's heart toward going and making disciples of all nations. Make disciple-making a regular rhythm in your home. Strive to raise your kids in a church-planting culture.

As our children transition from childhood to adulthood, let's aggressively pursue their transition from being hearers of the Word to doers of the Word. As God raises our kids to new life in Christ, let's raise them up to plant churches for the sake of his glory among the nations.

44

COVID COURAGE: A CALL FOR TRAINING CHURCH-PLANTING PASTORS

Bryan Laughlin

Planting and pastoring a church takes courage. Most sane people don't sign up to take a beating. Most folks don't charge into a storm. This is what shepherding is like under normal conditions. Yet now we're in the throes of COVID-19 where many of our sheep are scattered, confused, frustrated, wandering, and longing for hope and direction. This is a critical time for church leadership. Hirelings will just run when the race gets tough, cower in the face of challenge, and coddle rather than confront. Churches need courageous and persevering pastors to lead through this season, and they're formed in the field alongside other courageous leaders.

Pastoring is a hands-on applied science, not merely a speculative endeavor or a ministry management position. Those who work in the field develop strong hands and broad backs for lifting heavy loads. They understand how to break hard ground, till the soil, organize the field, plant seeds, water the garden, pull weeds, keep out pests, prune the young, and pick fruit. They've felt the scorching heat over many seasons, knowing that heat waves and droughts are "just another day" in the field of ministry.

Aspiring planters and pastors can only become these sorts of men when they're in the field co-laboring with other pastors. This is why God has called local church pastors to shepherd his flock (Acts 20:28) and train up other men (2 Tim. 2:2) to do likewise. This calling has four implications for training up planters and pastors.

1. Training Pastors Is the Responsibility of All Pastors

I serve as CEO of Grimké Seminary where our motto is, "Training pastors and planters in the church, by the church, for the church." Pastor training isn't an isolated academic endeavor; it's local church work. In a family, it's the parents' job to raise their children. Similarly, within the church, it's the pastors' job to raise up other pastors.

Too often pastors rely on "ministry-socialism" (waiting for someone else to train their next pastor) instead of "ministry-multiplication" (enjoying the task of raising up children in the faith to be the next leaders). Who is better qualified to identify and develop men from your flock to plant a church than you?

2. Training Pastors Is the Relational Ministry of Pastor

When I was following God's call toward pastoral ministry, I was kept at more than an arm's distance from my pastor. I never really had an opportunity to see behind the veil. I rarely got to simply walk, talk, and watch him navigate the rigors of daily pastoral ministry. For most church members, pastors seem to appear out of nowhere, providing no observable example of maturation to follow in the church.

Conversely, Jesus was with his disciples 24/7 so they could not merely hear the good news, but experience and dialogue about it, while seeing it lived out in his daily life. This is reflected in Paul's admonitions for churches to follow his example (1 Cor. 11:1). Training up pastors comes at a high personal cost, but its fruit is manifold and sweet.

3. Training Pastors Is a Shared Work with Other Pastors

Training planters and pastors is a collaborative work. It happens through the plurality of elders within a local church and alongside pastors of other faithful churches. God is the only one who can call men into the pastorate. It is, therefore, the complementary job of pastors together to recognize that call and to train those men accordingly.

This requires significant time with other pastors to observe the life and practice of aspiring planters. It means ensuring those being trained are taught by many seasoned practitioners who've made disciples in local churches and have borne lasting fruit. Erudite academics without calluses, pontificating planters without proof, and bloggers without buildings won't produce courageous pastors.

4. Training Pastors Is God's Work Through Pastors

Training pastors and planters is ultimately God's work. He gives us the audacity to pray boldly for him to call out future pastors and planters. He equips us to train faithful men to shepherd his church. God even provides the courage required to ask men to surrender their hopes, dreams, pursuits, careers, homes, security, and anything else that stands in the way of following him. He's always done it, and he'll continue to do it until he comes for us.

Our default instinct during COVID-19 is to hunker down and weather the storm, to wait for a more opportune time to get on with our mission. But our mission has never been more urgent. Christ is coming back, and many of our neighbors across the street and around the globe don't know him.

It's time for today's local church pastors to take responsibility for training the pastors and planters of tomorrow. More competent men are needed in the field, and it's our duty to prepare them. Seasons come and go, but our mission remains. So take courage, and train up.

45

PASTOR, EMBRACE THE CHANGING SEASONS OF MINISTRY

Bill Riedel

If you're a pastor, I don't have to tell you that ministry is demanding. There's sermon prep, counseling, managing staff, elders' meetings, overseeing the budget, visiting the sick, and more. It can feel overwhelming. And the pressure is only intensified in church planting.

But an essential component to all healthy pastoral ministry is the simple—yet weighty—charge Paul gives to the Ephesian elders: "Pay careful attention to yourselves and all the flock, of which the Holy Spirit has made you overseers, to care for the church of God, which he obtained with his own blood" (Acts 20:28).

How can church planters heed Paul's words, especially when there's so much else to do?

Blood-Bought

First, we'd do well to notice how the church is described in Acts 20:28: "the church of God, which he obtained with his own blood." The church itself is a beautiful portrait that manifests the gospel. We're hopeless on our own, but God intervened. Christ's blood purchased a people, rescuing them from slavery to sin and uniting them together as a family.

One important implication, therefore, is that we pastors care for *God's* church. It belongs to him, not us. He obtained it, and thus he ensures its ultimate good. The

Holy Spirit does appoint overseers to shepherd God's flock, but we would do well to embrace our role as those under the authority of the Chief Shepherd.

Shepherd's Seasons

As we labor to care for the sheep, there's much we can learn from actual shepherding work as a model for pastoral ministry. I've learned a lot from James Rebanks's book, *The Shepherd's Life*.[41] Ministry seasons can mirror seasons of the year, not necessarily in the actual calendar, but in the overall rhythms of a church's life.

For example, springtime is when "lambing" occurs, with lots of new life and heavy demands. It's when shepherds work hard to ensure the lambs get off to a good start. Similarly, the early days of planting a church can be as exhilarating as they are hectic and tiring. But it's only a season. If we perpetually live and work in ministry at the pace of the early days of planting, we will wear out the flock and destroy ourselves.

For shepherds, summer is a season of rest and preparation, in which hay is made for the coming year. In the same way, it's important to cultivate seasons of intentional rest for churches, purposefully slowing things down. We've adopted a rhythm we call "Family Sundays"—we give our ministry teams a break, all children join us throughout the service, and we have a shorter sermon from one of the elders. Not only does it help our church to rest, but it's also countercultural in the constant hustle of our city.

Autumn is when shepherds bring their sheep to competitions and auctions, and what they've worked hard for shows its value. I'm not suggesting there's an exact parallel to ministry here, but there are seasons in a church's life when long-planned strategies and hopes come to fruition. Celebration is an important discipline in caring well for the flock. The church-planting pastor should shepherd the church to give thanks to God, the Giver of every good and perfect gift (James 1:17).

---

[41] James Rebanks, *The Shepherd's Life: Modern Dispatches from an Ancient Landscape* (Flatiron Books, 2015).

Winter is a brutal time of suffering and hardship for shepherds. They suffer alongside the sheep, at times wondering whether they'll make it through. Pastors have a responsibility to care for the flock, especially when it's costly. This has been the hardest lesson for me to learn in planting a church. Most of the stories we hear are more triumphalist, which seem to leave little room for thinking about real suffering. The dark winter nights, whether in the church or in my own soul, are often the most difficult times to keep shepherding. But nothing builds greater trust in a church than a well-navigated "winter" as shepherds care for the sheep, enduring suffering with them while pointing to Jesus.

Respond to Needs

As the old saying goes, if your only tool is a hammer, everything starts to look like a nail. Often, the zeal of church planters doesn't reflect a full pastoral toolkit for meeting the needs of God's people. At times, especially early on, the weighty responsibility to care for people can lead to "hovering over" them, trying to micromanage their holiness and pursuit of Christ.

But we must remember that it's the Holy Spirit's job to change hearts, convict people of sin, and breathe life into weary souls. There will be times when a pastor's care for people calls for confrontation of sin in order to protect the unity and purity of the flock, and when wolves need to be fought off. Those fights are always costly.

There are also times when an angry sheep has an unseen wound that must be treated and cared for—when lethargy isn't laziness but an indicator of a deeper melancholy that needs an encouraging word to lift a downcast spirit. Pastors should also remember that not all opposition is personal; some is rooted in fears that can be addressed and cared for with a gentle word to take courage. As a shepherd has to know his sheep, so a pastor needs to know his people. Paul's call to the Thessalonians is helpful here: "And we urge you, brothers, admonish the idle, encourage the fainthearted, help the weak, be patient with them all" (1 Thess. 5:14).

Church-planting pastors must always remember that they are under-shepherds of the Lord Jesus Christ. The admonition to "pay careful attention to all the flock" is the essence of pastoral ministry, and therefore church planting. It's not an extraneous demand on top of the already full to-do list.

Even in the pressure-packed work of planting a church, remain focused on this high calling. Humbly press on and the Chief Shepherd himself will carry you through to an unfading reward.

46

6 WAYS CROSS-CULTURAL CHURCH PLANTING HAS BEEN GOOD FOR OUR KIDS

Jen Oshman

When we recently unpacked our boxes in suburban Denver, it was into my daughters' third home. But not only their third home, their third country. Third *continent*, actually. Third culture, third language, third way of life, third new beginning.

Though my husband and I are Colorado natives, we'd been gone a long time, and our kids had never lived here. As we met our new neighbors, they were either awestruck or incredulous. We heard, "Wow, what a great experience for your kids!" But also, "How sad. Didn't you want them to have roots somewhere?" Even those who did respond positively would often quietly whisper their concern: "How do you think they're handling it?"

By the time we moved back to the States with a gaggle of teens and preteens, we'd lived out the spectrum of great joys and deep sorrows in cross-cultural church planting. The joy of new believers and baptisms and discipleship was tempered by sorrow over our girls being bullied for being different. Not to mention the long, hard days in foreign schools with vastly different values from our own.

The skeptical neighbors weren't wrong. Our kids didn't have roots, at least not in the traditional sense.

Instead, their roots are global, established in the soil of the Great Commission. When we left America to make disciples of all nations, we trusted that Jesus would be with us always (Matt. 28:18–20). This promise was our bedrock then, and still is now. He's proven faithful to us and our children time and again. Cross-cultural church planting—though not without its challenges—has ultimately been a great gift to us.

Here are six things our kids—and our whole family—have learned.

1. Empathy

Our girls spent their formative years being "other." They didn't grasp the language, the inside jokes, or the nursery rhymes. But one beautiful gift of being an outsider is that you gain empathy for those who have known nothing else.

Overseas, they befriended the boy with autism, the girl whose parents neglected her, the Roma outcast. In our church plant in Denver, they're aware of visitors, kids new to youth group, and those hurting at school. God has given them compassionate hearts (Col. 3:12) toward outsiders, because they have walked in their shoes.

2. Christianity Is Diverse and Global

Having been a part of the church on three continents, our kids know that Christianity is not exclusively white and Western. They've participated in worship services ranging from wildly expressive to barely audible. They've experienced everything from high liturgy to flip-flops in the sanctuary. They know that within orthodoxy, there's a lot of room for difference. They've glimpsed God's work in a variety of tribes, tongues, and peoples (Rev. 7:9).

3. Where to Put Their Confidence

When I asked my girls to list some blessings from cross-cultural church planting, they all immediately said something like, "I'm brave," or "I'm flexible," or "I know God will help me." Their faith has been stretched—as has ours. They know we've only been willing to do hard things because God has enabled us to do so. They've labored in prayer and experienced Jesus with us in all the places we've called home.

4. The Church Is Family

Our children have known firsthand the truth of Christ's promise: "Everyone who has left houses or brothers or sisters or father or mother or children or lands, for my name's sake, will receive a hundredfold" (Matt. 19:29). While it's true no one can fill the shoes of our kids' biological grandmas, grandpas, aunts, uncles, and cousins, God did provide a hundredfold.

Other church planters and local Christians became aunties and uncles to my girls. We had friends we could call in the middle of the night, and brothers and sisters who laid down their lives for us. Our kids didn't lack relational support overseas, because God was faithful.

5. Home Is Not Here

As a family, we have a sense that there's no true home for us here on earth. No matter where we are, we feel a bit homesick—this awareness that we aren't *really* home, we don't *really* fit. With Paul, we say, "our citizenship is in heaven, and from it we await a Savior, the Lord Jesus Christ" (Phil. 3:20). One day we will enter our real home, where we will share a deep and unblemished connection with all who are gathered there.

6. Unity in Mission Fosters Joy

Here's perhaps the best gift: Being on mission together has fostered great joy in our family. In each country we've felt and prayed Paul's words: "We were ready to share with you not only the gospel of God but also our own selves, because you had become very dear to us" (1 Thess. 2:8). Our kids have truly partnered with us in loving nonbelievers and shining the light of Christ in dark places. This unity in mission has drawn us close to one another as we've labored and celebrated together.

In the early years of church planting, a mentor shared wise words with my husband and me: "Never sacrifice your family for the mission, but do sacrifice *as* a family *for* the mission."

There have been sacrifices. Our kids have paid a price. All cross-cultural church planters must count the cost.

Not every family can move overseas. Many are called to irreplaceable roles in their hometowns and local churches. But for those who sense that cross-cultural church planting might be for them, know this: Sacrificing as a family for the mission is costly, but Christ is worth it.

Jesus will provide a hundredfold—to you and to your children. He will indeed be with you, in every nation, to the end of the age.

47

WE SPENT OUR BEST YEARS OVERSEAS. AND THEY WERE HARD.

Jen Oshman

I'll never forget the agonized look on my mother-in-law's face when we said goodbye. Her years and life experience told her what we didn't yet know: Our move across the ocean would bring pain. Lots of it. We were heading overseas with her first newborn grandbaby, feeling like we were mere babies ourselves.

She knew there would be trials and hardships—and that we would endure them all 5,000 miles from home, family, and all things familiar. But we were propelled by optimism, God's calling, and an eager willingness to preach Christ among the unreached. Thus began our journey as cross-cultural church planters, first in Asia, later in Europe.

On the eve of that baby's sixteenth birthday, I'm looking back and can testify to two seemingly opposing truths: they were our best years, but they were hard years.

I've written before about the joys of raising children as cross-cultural church planters. It's true, if presented with a buffet of options for how to raise my kids again, I'd pick just that. In fact, I spend much of my days encouraging families to consider taking that plunge, and counseling and encouraging from afar those who already have. But the reality is, as numerous as the blessings are, so too are the causes for questioning and heartache.

The church—both those who go and those who send—

must acknowledge the hardships that cross-cultural workers face. And we must stand ready to help those who go as they walk through various valleys.

Difficulties for Families Serving Cross-Culturally

Here's a (by no means exhaustive) sampling of some of the afflictions:

- Traversing two or more cultures can prevent children from having a strong sense of identity and belonging. Also, the endless goodbyes with other expat families or with locals when the church planting family relocates can lead to loneliness and unprocessed grief.
- Being immersed in a highly secular setting can have a greater influence on a child than their parents' Christian influence. Kids might be exposed too early—and too often—to the realities of violence, poverty, sex trafficking, corruption, drugs and alcohol, and other dark, worldly trappings.
- Physical health may suffer, as access to good healthcare may be nonexistent or far away. Everything from a middle-of-the-night fever to scoliosis can morph into a major, life-altering crisis.
- Kids raised outside of their home countries don't get to know their cousins, aunts, uncles, grandparents, or the neighborhoods their parents grew up in. They face significant gaps in knowing about their home culture's norms (going "home" sure doesn't feel like it) and everyone misses out on the support of extended family in the formative years.
- Education is a constant concern. Learning in two languages is tough, not to mention dealing with special needs, keeping up with home country requirements, and navigating classmates' and teachers' expectations in a foreign country.
- While everyone says, "Kids are so resilient," the truth is they probably just don't have the words to express the grief they feel in living through

upheaval and uncertainty. Chances are their emotions are stuffed and saved for later. Many cross-cultural kids experience a season of processing trauma as young adults.

Heavy Burdens

Parents who are cross-cultural church planters must regularly ask if their situation inflicts undue physical, spiritual, or emotional harm on their children. How much is too much? What's simply part of the cost (Luke 14:28)? And how heavy must the burden be for a parent to determine that it's time to return home?

Cross-cultural workers weigh the answers to these questions constantly—they wonder if God is calling them to persist in trusting him by staying, or trust in him by going. Simply put, there's no easy way to measure the burdens and determine when the scale is tipped. Every family has a different capacity and calling. Every context has a different set of circumstances. Every local church, every church-planting team—and even every child—has a different threshold.

So how in the world can cross-cultural church-planting parents know when it's time to go (or stay)? How can we discern God's calling on us as parents when our children face hard things overseas? In short, we need wisdom from above. Thankfully, God promises to give us just that when we ask (James 1:5). And it comes primarily through his Word, his Spirit, and his people.

Seek Wisdom

It's a mystery—and certainly a unique process for everyone—but our heavenly Father communicates to us through the synthesis of his Word, his Spirit, and his people. These three means of grace complement one another and confirm God's calling on our lives and his leadership in our decisions.

Though often weary and overburdened, church planters must stay nourished by the words breathed out by God—they are there so that we might not be lacking anything (2 Tim. 3:16). Answers and wisdom for specific families and children may be sought out in the pages of the Bible. The Word is alive and active and can help us discern our motives in going or staying (Heb. 4:12).

Answers will likely come as the Spirit moves in our own consciences. Jesus said the Holy Spirit would be our helper, teacher, and peace giver (John 14:26, 27). The Holy Spirit will lead us as we lead our children.

And the message delivered through God's Word and pressed upon us by God's Spirit will be confirmed by God's people. It's imperative that we gather with our siblings in Christ so that we might be strengthened by accountability (Gal. 6:1–5) as we build one another up (1 Thess. 5:11). Often other Christians can see things in us and our families that we cannot see in ourselves. Input from teammates, team leaders, and other Christians is invaluable for the family living and serving cross-culturally.

All Things for Good

Cross-cultural church-planting parents can lean on wisdom received through these three supernatural resources as they discern God's leading for their children. And we can lean confidently, knowing that God is sovereign. We need not be paralyzed by fear and uncertainty. We may boldly go—or stay—knowing that God is on his throne and he works all things (even perceived mistakes or misunderstandings) for our good (Rom. 8:28). God's plans, even for church plants in unreached places—and for families serving therein—cannot be thwarted (Isa. 14:27).

Yes, the burdens of the family serving cross-culturally can be many. The pain that my mother-in-law expressed was ultimately realized ten years later when she languished and died from ALS. Due to immigration laws preventing our adopted daughter from entering the United States, we could only watch and weep from across the world. God's Word, Spirit, and people upheld us in our grief.

As we've experienced ourselves and with so many others, in addition to the joy, the years of cross-cultural church planting can be challenging. But God promises to be our ever-present help in times of trouble (Ps. 46:1). The

Lord will help you and me and every church planter in every nation, as we seek to serve him, grow his church, and minister to our children.

He is near. He is there in his Word, his Spirit, and his people. Church planter, pursue these three humble means of grace as if your life and the life of your children depend on it. Because they do.

48

AN UNEXPECTED STRATEGY FOR REACHING THE MUSLIM WORLD

Landon Dennis

The Muslim world has seen its share of missionaries throughout history. Many faithful men and women have left hearth and home and given their lives to see the Middle East evangelized. We praise God for these brothers and sisters.

And while that's true, there remains immense gospel need in this part of the world. I believe there is something lacking in our efforts to reach the Muslim world—and that thing is often faithful, gospel-preaching churches. At one level, this is understandable given the historical realities of the region. But this part of the world is changing such that this need no longer be the case.

I've yet to meet a missionary here who doesn't share my desire to see churches planted among the unreached—specifically Muslims. But for most, this seems to be a distant dream—a prize yet to be obtained, maybe only just visible on the horizon of the future.

In most cases today, churches are being planted only after years, if not decades, of evangelism and discipleship. In the current state of affairs, the church tends to follow as a consequence of the gospel instead of an attractive and compelling argument for it.

I'm not suggesting that we abandon the traditional missions strategies: doing the hard work of learning language, connecting with local people, and sharing the gospel in the context of relationship. We must continue doing this (often slow) work in difficult places. But I am suggesting that we add something to that strategy.

We have a God-ordained missional instrument to make the gospel of Christ known in the Muslim world. Her name is the bride of Christ. I'm not speaking simply from theological conviction, though I'm convinced the concept is biblical. I've also witnessed such things.

Neglected Instrument

A few years ago, a church-planting team was sent out from an existing church here on the Arabian Peninsula. I had the privilege of leading this team. We were sent by an English-speaking church in this region to plant another English-speaking church here. Most of us didn't learn Arabic, nor any trendy new evangelism strategies. We simply went with the ambition to be the church.

To this day, we gather together weekly around the Word of God—we preach, sing, and pray it. We strive to love one another by the Spirit's power. We bear one another's burdens, mourn one another's losses, and rejoice in one another's victories. We don't divide ourselves by ethnic, racial, or socioeconomic differences, but unite around our great commonality: Jesus Christ.

This is nothing radical or new. But guess what? People notice.

I've sat with many seekers and not-yet-believers during my time in Arabia, a number of them Muslims. The consistent thing that drew them into gospel conversation has been the church—a community comprising dozens of nationalities from every economic level loving one another and pursuing Jesus together. It's simple, yet beautiful. This is exactly what the gospel does. It creates unity in diversity. But I fear it's a missional instrument we too often neglect.

Global World, Global Church

Many assume that Muslim nations are closed to an overt Christian witness. And yes, there are predominately Muslim countries largely closed to Christians. I'm not ignoring that problem. But there are also many nations where Christians are largely free to gather and worship Christ. This is true in places like Bahrain, Kuwait, Oman, Qatar, and the United Arab Emirates.

In an increasingly global and urban world, the local church—meeting primarily in a trade language like English—offers real benefits to our mission strategy among Muslims. A strategy we hope will ultimately lead to the planting of healthy, sustainable Arabic-speaking churches. Here are a few things the local church does.

1. Models the inclusivity of the gospel

I've heard people liken the cities of the Arabian Peninsula to a (poorly) tossed salad. Unlike a mixing pot, people stay in their clumps. Tomatoes stay with tomatoes, carrots with carrots, cucumbers with cucumbers, and so on. This is generally true.

Although this oil-rich peninsula has gathered people from every corner of the earth, most have remained neatly divided along ethnic and economic lines. Racism, classism, and inequality are largely accepted as part of life here—diversity and integration don't just "happen." But in the local church, the gospel's power shines as these divides are abolished in Christ.

One of the first Muslim-background men we saw turn to Christ had come to the peninsula assuming he'd find solidarity with his Muslim brothers. The opposite proved true. He wasn't from the "right" country or class, and this deficiency was clearly communicated to him, even in the mosque. He was devalued and excluded.

But then he met the church. He saw a community where men and women, black and white, rich and poor, were all treated with dignity. All were equally loved—not on the basis of their identity or heritage, but on the basis of Christ's finished work on their behalf. It wasn't that our brother was just *told* that all were welcome; he *saw* and experienced that welcome, and it changed his life.

2. Demonstrates Sprit-filled community

Whether in corporate worship or personal

relationships, Christian community depends on the Holy Spirit. In Ephesians 5, Paul exhorts believers to be filled with the Holy Spirit—which results in our singing to one another, our giving thanks to God, and our mutual submission (Eph. 5:18–21). How will we display these things to the nations unless we are gathered together in the church?

An Arab friend looked at me after we read Acts 4 together and said, "Next time we get together, tell me about your church." A little confused, I asked what he meant. He answered, "You Christians have something different. I go to the mosque. We have a community. But when I visited your church, I saw something altogether different. The way you relate to and love one another is unique. I sense you have something we don't, and I want you to tell me about it." Friend, his name is the Holy Spirit.

3. Mobilizes Christians for mission

I love missionaries. I love that many men and women have left the comforts of their homeland and crossed cultures to share the gospel with the least reached. Their stories encourage our souls. But there are still so few. In reality, those willing to go are limited, as are the financial resources to send them. What if we could equip the Christians already living among the least-reached to do the work of mission through the local church?

One African brother came to the peninsula to find work. He was a young Christian when we met him, with little concern for God's mission. But God began to grow him. Over time, he came to see the connection between his faith and his vocation: He was working in a place where very few people knew Jesus. Shortly thereafter, this brother began bringing a Muslim co-worker to church. Hardly a week goes by without both of them sitting there as the gospel is preached.

Now, this brother didn't have to go through formal training or raise funds. He doesn't have a list of partner churches. But he is active in the work of missions among the unreached. Even better, there are thousands like him who, if they were connected to a healthy church and discipled well, could be mobilized for the spread of the gospel on the Arabian Peninsula and beyond.

Let's not wait to introduce the world—and yes, the Muslim world—to the church. Let's plant churches that plant churches to this end.

49

CHURCH-PLANTING MOMENTUM IN INDIA

Christy Britton

The Acts 29 Emerging Regions Network serves in places where Christians are few, churches are under-resourced, and persecution is severe. Will Bostian, lead pastor of City Church Fort Worth, writes, "Not everyone can be in these places. This is why we aim to facilitate partnerships *between* churches to *plant churches*—specifically in unreached areas."

India is one of the most unreached places in the world. It's home to 1.3 billion people, ninety percent of whom practice Hinduism. The need for gospel proclamation is staggering in this theologically impoverished nation. Reaching these people for God's glory requires great sacrifice, perseverance, trust, and collaboration.

Despite complications from a global pandemic, unrest, and opposition, Jesus is growing his church in India. He's rescuing rebels from their sin and adopting them as beloved children. Church-planting momentum is building in India, and it's our privilege to be God's fellow workers (1 Cor. 3:9) as we labor alongside him and others who have a passion to see the people of India worship the risen Christ.

India Catalyst

Partnership is essential to any church-planting strategy. We depend on one another as we work together to multiply our efforts. One man who is passionate about building global partnerships is Jeff Neville. Jeff serves as the India Catalyst for Emerging Regions in Acts 29. Jeff (a father to nine kids!) has been a planter and pastor for 13 years. For 10 years, he led Red Tree Church in St. Louis, Missouri, to partner with a church in Mumbai, India.

After much traveling back and forth between St. Louis and Mumbai, he eventually moved to Mumbai to invest in church planters who were starved for theological training and collaboration. While there, he established partnerships with Redeemer City to City, the International Mission Board, and Acts 29. He developed a one-year cohort for 15 aspiring planters. These men are all currently engaged in some capacity in planting churches across India.

For the past eighteen months, Jeff has been involved in replanting an Acts 29 church in St. Louis. With a core group of forty, this church has tripled in size—even amid the pandemic. Heartland Church joins Jeff in his passion for the people of India to know and worship Christ. Jeff is invested in the church-planting momentum that's building in India and strives to launch others into this great work God is accomplishing.

Indian Convert

God is raising up men and women in India to reach lost people within their own country. Vihaan was an imam, serving at a mosque in Mumbai. His family are all Muslim clerics (father, uncles, brothers). In May of 2018, Vihaan met Jeff and Saju (an Acts 29 candidate pastor) at a mall in Mumbai. He told them he was reading the Bible to better understand the Christian faith and lead his people through their questions about Christianity.

Over the course of several meetings, Jeff and Saju walked him through the gospel and Vihaan professed faith in Jesus. A week later, they baptized him where he publicly shared his testimony to a crowd of believers. Jeff and Saju discipled Vihaan for the next year, teaching him the truths of Scripture. He was even able to attend a few church-planting conferences.

Vihaan has suffered great persecution since becoming

a follower of Christ. Despite threats to his life, and to the lives of his parents, he has a strong desire to take the gospel to the Muslim community in Mumbai, and to impact India for the sake of Christ.

India's Future

A year ago, there were three Acts 29 member churches in India, and all of them were planted over a decade ago. Today, there are four member churches, four candidate churches, and 13 planters in the pipeline. In February of this year (2020), just before the coronavirus exploded around the world, 100 pastors and aspiring planters from India gathered in Mumbai for the Acts 29 India National Summit.

Jeff believes in the next three years we'll have a dozen or more Acts 29 churches planted in India, and that they'll become their own network. He says India is positioned to become the largest, most influential sending nation in the world.

God is mightily moving in India. He's building his church and we get to be part of it. Is it difficult? Yes. Is it costly? Very. Is it worth it? Absolutely. The difficulty of the task doesn't deter us from it.

God sends us to *all* nations to make disciples. Even the hard ones. But we can go with confidence because he's promised to be with us when we do (Matt. 28:19–20). Let's work together to see churches planted, collaborative networks launched, and Jesus worshiped to the ends of the earth!

50

CANADA'S FORGOTTEN UNREACHED

Amy Tyson

Perched on the edge of the vast Atlantic Ocean, the city of St. John's, Newfoundland, is over 500 years old. The province of Newfoundland and Labrador overflows with pristine beauty—pure air, sparkling water—and abundant natural resources. Acts 29 pastor Steve Bray calls it a province of whales, icebergs, and fishing. "When John Cabot discovered Newfoundland in 1497," he said, "the cod was so plentiful it shimmered on the sea."

Today, the oil and gas industry has brought new prosperity to the province. But economic growth can't offer lasting hope to the 525,000 souls in this massive and remote land.

If Anchorage and Las Vegas Had A Baby

The island of Newfoundland is geographically separated from the rest of the country, and with the oil boom, people can make a lot of money quickly. This equals isolation, big-paying jobs, and idleness—a dangerous combination.

Steve Bray pastors Calvary Baptist Church in St. John's. He describes his city by asking people to "imagine if Anchorage and Las Vegas had a child."

"We spend more money per capita than anybody in Canada a year on alcohol," he said, "and we have the highest rate of sexually transmitted diseases." One of the largest Roman Catholic sex scandals happened in

Newfoundland.[42] In this troubled and lonely society, there's almost no evangelical witness.

Hard Ground

In Canada, there's a commendable missionary focus on First Nations—indigenous peoples who have no access to the gospel or who have been hurt by the misguided missionary efforts of previous generations. This gospel work gets good publicity, as it should.

But Steve Bray says that the western-heritage people of Newfoundland are the forgotten unreached. "Nobody even knows that there's this city of a quarter of a million people, and not even 2,000 broadly evangelical Christians."

The city of St. John's makes up almost half of the entire population of the hulking 156,453 square-mile area of Newfoundland and Labrador. Less than one percent of the total population of St. John's attends *any* type of evangelical church, with the five denominations being Roman Catholic, Pentecostal, Salvation Army, Anglican, and United (a watered-down combination of Methodism, Congregationalism, and Presbyterianism).

Until about the 1970s, Baptist churches were considered cults. As reformed, complementarian Baptists, Steve calls Calvary Baptist Church "an absolute enigma" in the culture.

This is stony ground, and the cultural context makes evangelism difficult. Newfoundlanders are hospitable and welcoming, but skeptical. Almost every evangelical church-planting effort led by outsiders has failed.

Mile One Mission

By God's grace, Calvary Baptist aims to do something about all this. They believe the answer is planting lots of healthy local churches. Through links with Acts 29's Church in Hard Places pastors, Stephen Bray connected with Mez McConnell and 20schemes, a church-planting

---

[42] "At least 26 civil cases of clergy abuse still open in N.L.," *CBC News*, Feb 21, 2019: https://www.cbc.ca/news/canada/newfoundland-labrador/catholic-church-clergy-abuse-st-johns-1.5028276 accessed on Jan 29, 2021.

initiative among Scotland's urban poor. He visited Scotland, observed striking similarities in culture, and brought back a new vision for evangelism.

Instead of seeking to grow the single congregation of Calvary Baptist numerically, Calvary Baptist wants to see many local neighborhood churches planted all around St. John's and beyond. This is the heartbeat of Mile One Mission. Steve asked his elders, "What would be better for St John's: one church of 1,000, or ten churches of 100 who are networked together, but spread around the city?"

They aim to be distinct congregations in their different neighborhoods—involved in their communities, supporting local businesses, and knowing and loving their neighbors as they extend the saving gospel of Jesus.

The vision isn't limited to St. John's. Mile One Mission aims to plant ten churches strategically in neighborhoods across St. John's and then across the island. Recent developments even include two locations in Labrador, far to the north. "If St. John's is a church in a hard place," Steve said, "that's a church in no place."

Steve hopes that the ministry training available through Mile One Mission—church planter residencies and internships—will be a catalyst for mission in Newfoundland, as well as a resource for those just starting in ministry. Mile One Mission, 20schemes, and Acts 29 are working alongside one another as partners in church planting. There are even talks about Mile One Mission becoming an incubator through which Newfoundland can send people to Ireland!

Waves of cultural change that hit other parts of the world don't often get to Newfoundland, being an island. But if a cultural trend does make it there, it can become something powerfully compelling. Steve is praying for the good news of Jesus to establish deep, fruitful roots.

"Please pray," Steve said, "for gospel communities of light to grow throughout this land, with believers who are 'all in' spreading Jesus's message of hope."

51

THE ADVANCING CHURCH IN BURKINA FASO

Travis Whitehead

Nestled between the sandy landscapes of the Sahara Desert and the deep forests of West Africa, the people of Burkina Faso have experienced great devastation in 2020. They've been one of the hardest-hit countries in Africa by the coronavirus. Violence from extremist groups like Boko Haram and Al Qaeda has displaced over a million people from their homes. Children are unable to safely attend school, and famine and poverty abound.

Against this backdrop of uncertainty, sickness, and violence, the gospel of Jesus Christ advances.

Acts 29 is a global family laboring together to plant church-planting churches that proclaim the name of Jesus in all places. Suffering and opposition are plentiful in Burkina Faso, but Jesus builds his church as we go and make disciples of all nations.

The scope of the Great Commission can be overwhelming. God tells us to take the gospel to *everyone, everywhere*. But in the face of the sheer size and difficulty of this task, Jesus gives us a promise: "I will build my church and the gates of hell will not prevail against it" (Matt 16:18).

Pastor Training

Acts 29 church planter, Marcel Yanogo, pastors Temple Philadelphie in Ouagadougou, Burkina Faso. Marcel also leads a Bible school (Verse by Verse) in northern Burkina, equipping church planters for ministry. Marcel launched the school in 2006, recognizing the great need for the gospel to be proclaimed in his country. He sold his motorcycle, bought a piece of land with the proceeds, and began equipping pastors.

Today, over 100 pastors and aspiring planters participate in the training program. For a few days a week over several months, they learn how to read, understand, apply, and teach the Bible—book by book, verse by verse. With very little biblical literacy present in the country and scarce access to training resources, this type of foundational training is essential for the church in Burkina Faso to flourish.

Gospel Partnerships

Like most stories of the gospel advancing in difficult places, Marcel's efforts have been strengthened by partners. Making disciples in places where Jesus is neither known nor worshiped is collaborative work, and God is raising up men and women all over the world to accomplish this task. And he invites more to become fellow workers (3 John 8).

Shortly after opening the school, Marcel met Loren Anderson, an Acts 29 church planter from Bend, Oregon, through a mutual acquaintance. Over the next few years, Loren and Marcel struck up a friendship, and The Fellowship at Bend Church began directing most of their missions fund to support pastor training in Burkina through Verse by Verse.

Loren and Marcel talk almost every week, praying for the Holy Spirit to move among the Burkina people. Loren is the first to say he's not an expert on the various peoples or cultures of Burkina Faso. Still, believers in Oregon are overjoyed to partner with believers in tiny towns and brushlands in northern Burkina Faso to make more disciples. And as the gospel advances, enemies become brothers and sisters through the blood of Jesus, and churches are planted despite the devil's relentless efforts to subdue them.

Prevailing Churches

In the last 14 years, the men trained at Verse by Verse have planted more than 100 churches in areas of Burkina occupied by extremist groups hostile to Christianity. Despite constant persecution in the northern parts of the country, Burkina Faso believers are growing in their understanding of God's Word. And as they apply and proclaim it, the Holy Spirit is cultivating bold believers whose confidence in Jesus is a compelling witness and invitation to "come and see." Marcel says, "We want the persecution to end. But the gospel and witness in persecution is being used by God."

One day, a multitude from every nation, from all tribes and peoples and languages, will gather in heaven to praise the God of our salvation (Rev. 5:9–10; 7:9). Until then, God is redeeming and raising up faithful men and women across the world to boldly proclaim the good news of salvation to men and women who are desperate to hear it.

Jesus has given all believers a mandate to be part of his kingdom's advancement. So we go and we send with hopeful confidence. And in this kingdom, the Holy Spirit works through bold proclamation, faithful sending, and gospel partnerships like we see taking place in Bend, Oregon, and Ouagadougou, Burkina Faso.

Christ commissions us to take the gospel to all places, and he emboldens us with the promise of his presence. So let us go with courage and confidence. And let us go together as fellow workers.

52

DIVERSITY THE WORLD CAN'T ACHIEVE

Doug Logan

Leonardo da Vinci wrote, "Iron rusts from disuse; stagnant water loses its purity, and in cold weather becomes frozen; even so does inaction sap the vigors of the mind."

The same is true for the church.

If abandoned to being a stagnant pool, it will quickly lose its purity and vitality as it becomes polluted with narrow, self-serving homogeneity.

Plan

God's plan has always been to reach ends of the earth with his message of hope and forgiveness. We can trace this plan from the first gospel glimpse in Genesis 3:15, through God's promises to the Israelites, culminating in the promised Messiah—and right down to today, seen in the ever-expanding body of Christ. Church planting puts the glory of God on display as it creates new communities that reflect the diversity of his creation.

If we are to see biblical diversity, then we must labor to see the gospel spread to all people. And this gospel message is transformative. Let me suggest a twofold framework: gospel imperative and missional imperative.

Gospel

The gospel imperative is foundational to a biblical expression of diversity, because it builds on the redemptive work of Jesus Christ. As Jesus declared, "I say to you that you are Peter, and on this rock I will build my church, and the gates of hell will not overpower it" (Matt. 16:18).

This promise from Christ gives us all the confidence we need. His church will be built—against all odds, no matter the cost, in the face of sinful rebellion and satanic onslaught. Coupled with this great promise are commands that inform the life of God's people. "What is the greatest commandment?" the antagonistic Pharisees asked Jesus. He replied:

> Love the Lord your God with all your heart, with all your soul, and with all your mind. This is the greatest and most important command. The second is like it: Love your neighbor as yourself. All the Law and the Prophets depend on these two commands. (Matt. 22:37–38)

Jesus was dead against first-century Jewish exclusivity. The people *of* God must be united in love *for* God—which is expressed in how we love our neighbor. Love for God fuels love for neighbor.

The gospel imperative, then, is the catalyst for the missional imperative: "Go, therefore, and make disciples of all nations" (Matt. 28:19). We cannot be content in the stagnant pool of self-made individualism. We must go, bringing the fresh water of the gospel to all nations.

As the gospel spreads through the witness of God's people, the diversity of the church comes alive and flourishes in every local expression of Christ's body.

Mission

The gospel imperative and missional imperative fulfill what God promised in the Old Testament. Jesus championed the diversity of God's new family. And the book of Revelation brings heaven's plan to its crescendo:

> After this I looked, and there was a vast multitude from every nation, tribe, people, and language, which no one could number, standing before the throne and before the Lamb. They were clothed in white robes with palm branches in their hands. And they cried out in a

> loud voice: Salvation belongs to our God, who is seated on the throne, and to the Lamb! (Rev. 7:9–10)

We cannot overstate the significance of Revelation 7. This will happen. The diversity we long for—or should long for—will be achieved.

By God's grace, we've seen this happen in our church in Camden, New Jersey. We haven't devised a clever formula or strategy. We haven't done anything particularly special. What we have done is *prayed* and *acted*.

One thing we've done is call our people to *move* into—not just visit—specific neighborhoods. One such area is Cramer Hill, whose population is more than 70 percent Latino and nearly 25 percent African American. We've sent people into Cramer Hill with gospel intentionality; and by God's grace, we've seen many from the area put their faith in Christ.

For many years, we held our annual church Christmas party in the home of one of our suburban members. We invited people from the hood and the suburbs; many of these folks have never meaningfully interacted with the other group in their lives. They've never had reason to rub shoulders with people so unlike them. But because of the gospel, we had upper-middle-class Christians alongside Christians who live in the hood, both groups intentionally bringing their unbelieving friends together. It was remarkable. But then again, that's what the gospel does.

True Diversity

The world imagines it will see diversity spring from a culture that promotes individualism. But true diversity will only come as we die to ourselves and prefer the needs of others. We must re-evaluate our personal preferences, political leanings, socioeconomic status—indeed, our very lives—in light of the gospel of Jesus Christ.

As the people of God, we ought to intentionally pursue diversity—meaningful diversity. How do we do that? We plant churches.

Jesus died to purchase a diverse people; why wouldn't we pursue that now? Yes, there will be challenges. Yes, we will make mistakes. No, it won't be easy. But it will be worth it.

May we never yawn at something for which our Savior bled. Instead, may we labor and long for the future that awaits us: the most diverse community in the history of the world, gathered as one around the throne of the Lamb.

53

IS YOUR CHURCH (POLITICALLY) DIVERSE?

Bill Riedel

Partisan politics creates dividing walls that can feel impenetrable.

Seven years ago, we planted a church in the heart of Washington D.C. We meet in a historic building four blocks from the U.S. Capitol building. While we have our fair share of politicos on both sides of the aisle, we also have folks who work in media, communications, education, defense, non-profits, coffee shops, and many other jobs you'd find in any other city.

National attention is always focused on the individuals voted into office and sent here to work, but our primary focus is the people who call D.C. *home*. There's more to life here than party lines.

We can't escape politics, however—nor do most of our people want to. Political engagement is important, especially for Christians in positions where they have to work out gospel-informed values for the good of all people (this includes those on both left and right).

In many ways D.C. is comparable to ancient Athens, filled with those who "spend their time in nothing except telling or hearing something new" (Acts 17:21). The picture of people discussing ideology in the marketplace, with idolatry on full display through monuments and cultural temples, is familiar.

From the beginning, we've prayed and worked toward political diversity in our church. And praise God, our church is politically diverse. But the past few years have pulled back the curtain on deepening divides that have affected churches across America.

In the midst of a right focus on the need for diversity in churches, and particularly in new church plants, one often-neglected consideration is political ideology. Remember that Jesus had a zealot and a tax collector in the same group of disciples. It doesn't get much more politically diverse.

Here are six lessons we've learned in planting and cultivating a politically diverse church.

1. Open and Closed Hand

It is essential to establish the "closed hand" issues to which the church will cling and members submit. We lay these out in our statement of faith.

At the same time, it is just as important to establish "open hand" issues. These are secondary/tertiary theological and philosophical matters—which may include certain beliefs and practices of the church—but where diversity is allowed within the membership's views.

We've found that we need to be more explicit about the things the church is *unwilling* to fight and divide over. We celebrate the diversity of our church openly in membership classes and members' meetings, and we make it clear that divisions over open-hand matters have no place in the church (and could even be cause for church discipline).

As for politics, there is no place for partisan platforms or division in the church, nor diminishing other members because of their ideological perspectives. From the beginning of a church plant, it is crucial to establish your open- and closed-hand commitments with clarity. Otherwise, you can expect those who join to have their own plans for where the church will stand.

2. Don't Avoid Political Issues

This is probably the most tempting mistake for a church-planting pastor. Churches have too often tried to cultivate political diversity by avoiding politics altogether or thinking they can be apolitical and "just preach the gospel." But contentious times will expose the anemia of that approach.

Christ's kingdom is inherently political. Now, we hear "political" and immediately think "partisan." But Christ's kingdom is political without being partisan.

It's unwise to chase the news cycle, but it's pastorally irresponsible to avoid applying God's Word to the issues God's people face in their lives.

3. Dismantle Partisan Narratives

As James Davison Hunter wisely observes, "Politics is always a crude simplification of public life, and the common good is always more than its political expression."[43] It takes a lot of work to get underneath partisan narratives and drive toward nuanced truth, especially in a society that perpetuates polarized simplicity.

We must do the hard work to show that partisan rhetoric falls short. There's a greater vision of hope and justice. Biblical Christianity doesn't fit neatly into any partisan platform.

In D.C., we challenge people to stay engaged in political work and even within parties, but with a clear view to the shortfalls of the "gospels" each party preaches.

4. Preach God's Word and Christ as King

Stick closely to the authority and sufficiency of Scripture. Apply it to real-life issues. Scripture doesn't avoid the hard realities of life or the brokenness of this world but casts a vision for God's work of renewing and restoring all things.

The congregation needs a regular reminder that Jesus is King over all—and that he has no political party. As Mark Dever has said, "The Jesus we share is more important than the politics we don't." This emphasis is especially important as a church is planted. We must pursue unity under Jesus our King.

---

[43] James Davison Hunter, *To Change the World: The Irony, Tragedy, and Possibility of Christianity in the Late Modern World* (Oxford University Press, 2010), 185.

5. Lay Down Personal Rights for the Sake of the Gospel

The apostle Paul did this (1 Cor. 9). It is unnecessary and unhelpful to demand all Christians lay down the right to partisan political involvement and investment. We need Christians engaged in politics.

As a pastor, though, the unity of the church and the advance of the gospel across partisan lines are worth relinquishing this right. The harder it is for your people to figure out how you vote, the better you can serve them and challenge their ideology.

6. Pray for Unity in the Spirit

There are countless ways a church plant can get sidetracked or fractured. The contentiousness and rhetoric of political divisions can wreak havoc in churches. It takes a miraculous movement of the Spirit to bring unity across dividing walls of hostility. The good news is that's exactly what the Spirit does, as we all fix our eyes on Jesus Christ.

Navigating partisan divides can feel overwhelming, and they're dangerous when they seep into the church. Church plants have the opportunity to shape a culture, from the outset, that depends on the sufficiency of the gospel and a devotion to Jesus as our only King.

We have the privilege of equipping our members to work for the good of people and the glory of Christ across party lines. Let's plant churches, then, that expose the temptation to find justification in political affiliation—and instead proclaim the hope that comes only by grace through faith in King Jesus.

54

CULTIVATING UNITY IN DIVERSITY IN YOUR CHURCH PLANT

Badi Badibanga

As an avid rugby fan, I'm enjoying the Rugby World Cup. In the run-up to this year's cup, fans and experts alike speculated on various factors—from team rosters to weather conditions—as they tried to predict whether their nation would succeed. We'll have to wait to see who comes out victorious.

There is one factor, however, that gets overlooked in these debates—and that is crucial to success.

Few things will spoil a team's chances at victory like a lack of unity. Don't get me wrong: superb talent, hard work, and excellent coaching are vital. But even with these things, disunity kills. It's like a poison flowing through a team's veins.

Corporate Unity

I recently received a call from a pastor who's planting a church in the same area as ours. He wanted to extend me the courtesy of telling us their plans. I felt deeply honored that he'd consider us even though we'd never met.

As we talked, he asked if we could meet up, expressing a desire to glean whatever wisdom I may have to offer. I agreed, despite being reluctant to share my "wisdom." I often feel as though we're fumbling our way through ministry, simply asking God to keep us faithful. As I put down the phone, I pondered what I'd just committed to. *Am I in over my head? Will I actually have anything of value to say to this brother?*

But as I prayed before our conversation, I sensed that I should encourage their team to cultivate unity in diversity—not just in their core team, but in the church as a whole. Here are three things they—and anyone else involved in church planting—can do to cultivate unity in diversity.

1. Vision

When I worked in student ministry, my regional director would say that "vision leaks." It's imperative, then, to keep reminding people of the vision so they won't stray from it.

Having served in various ministries, I've also learned that "vision morphs and scales." So it's essential to keep adapting as a team in order to attack new horizons that a growing vision will make available.

To be clear, what I mean by vision is simply how we, as God's people, apply the biblical marks of the church within our local context. Staying united in this vision is therefore crucial. It can be tempting to leave such a vision behind if your church grows numerically. When such growth happens, it's all too easy for pragmatism to creep in. People end up relying on "what works"—even if it means leaving the original vision by the wayside.

Healthy church-planting teams cultivate unity in the biblical vision they begin with, so that the "success" (or lack thereof) they experience doesn't lead them down selfish paths of pragmatic pursuits.

2. Mission and contribution

If it's important to cultivate unity in diversity around the vision we're heading toward, the same should apply to *how* we get there: namely, the mission.

Critical to any sports team's success is their ability to execute, as a unit, on the game plan. It's not enough for the players to merely *know* the plan; they must embrace it wholeheartedly.

That said, an effective team will cultivate the *necessary*

levels of buy-in from its members. When it comes to a core team in church planting, different members will contribute at different levels. The contribution of the lead planter will look different from the young professional on call at work, which will in turn look different from the mother of four. Nevertheless, each of these people can work together for the sake of the church's mission (evangelism and discipleship) at their diverse levels of capacity. Their buy-in is equal, but their contribution is different.

Cultivating buy-in for the mission, with healthy levels of expectation from each team member, accounts for the kind of "every-member ministry" rooted in a healthy understanding of the church as the body of Christ (1 Cor. 12:12–31).

3. Appreciation

There's a difference between valuing what someone has to give and actually *enjoying* their contribution. The latter is what I mean by appreciation. It's good to tell someone they're needed; but do they also feel wanted?

If we let people know they're loved and enjoyed—both for who they are and what they bring—they're far more likely to contribute wholeheartedly over the long haul. Cultivating unity in diversity works toward ensuring that people feel appreciated as they labor for God's glory.

No Guarantee

The diversity of gifting within church-planting teams doesn't guarantee success. But we know that unity in diversity honors God, regardless of the results. How we cultivate it, then, matters immensely.

We can trust God to work through his Word and through his people in his world. May his Spirit empower us to cultivate unity in diversity within the teams we lead and serve with. This will surely benefit the churches we plant and the people we long to know and worship Christ.

55

HOW TO PREPARE TO PLANT A CHURCH AMONG THE POOR

Mez McConnell

Many church planters and established pastors wonder how they're going to get started when they're on their own or have few resources. Several folks have visited the church I pastor—Niddrie Community Church in Edinburgh, Scotland—and commented that it's easier for us because we have a team. But no one else was working full-time when I began the work.[44]

So I tell guys to start with the raw material you have and work from there. If you're on your own and starting from scratch, then pray for others to join you. Don't rush. Choose team members carefully and be sure they understand your vision and direction. If you're an experienced pastor, offer an internship to existing members or recruit from seminaries or other local churches.

Maybe we don't have because we haven't consistently asked our heavenly Father. This is sure: change will not come if we are not willing to take steps of faith.

Don't Be Tied to One Model

Some people are passionate about one particular model for church planting and revitalizing, as if the job is best done the same way every time. But in my experience, there are a lot of good ways to go about it. For example:

---

[44] This article is an adapted excerpt from *Church in Hard Places: How the Local Church Brings Life to the Poor and Needy* (Crossway, 2016).

- In Brazil, I started with a group of eight men and women. We met daily for a year, studying, praying, eating, and doing ministry on the streets together. When the time came to start a work in our favela, we knew each other well, and we hit the ground running. The church grew quickly.
- In Niddrie, Scotland, I inherited a group, so I had to go about re-educating them, largely from the pulpit. I invested more time with those who seemed like they resonated with the new vision for ministry. It's been a different way of doing church, but it's slowly becoming effective.
- In an Edinburgh scheme called Gracemount, we have a young couple who started a church from scratch. They began with contacts through a local parachurch ministry, and now there's an established church shining gospel light in a spiritually dark place.

The point is that there is no one perfect way to do church planting and revitalizing. Every location is different and presents different opportunities. A trailer park might require a different strategy than an urban housing project, both of which might be different from a church plant in the suburbs.

If you're tied to one model, you may miss a good opportunity. And if you import your model into a different location without taking into account its culture and needs, you're asking for trouble.

Be Realistic About the Financial Cost

Two young men made an appointment to meet in my office to talk about their vision of working with gangs in South Africa. When I asked how much money they were hoping to raise, the answer was naively low. They'd apparently planned to live on a shoestring budget without factoring in rent, a car, fuel, a work fund, trips home, medical expenses, and a little luxury called food. They had absolutely no clue about the true costs associated with planting or revitalizing churches in poor areas.

The average Western church-planting strategy plans

for financial independence in three to five years. That is extremely unrealistic in poor communities, where fiscal independence may take a decade or more. New ministries to the poor require long-term financing. Thinking carefully about finances can help protect the church planter from worry, preoccupation, and anxiety.

The difficulty of financing a church in poor areas is one reason why churches everywhere should join or develop a close network with other churches. Together they can financially and spiritually support the work of churches in poorer areas. If you're part of an affluent church looking to help see the gospel spread among the poor, it may be that the most effective way for your congregation to participate is through financial support.

We also need to cultivate individual donors who understand and appreciate our ministry context. Sadly, such people are in short supply in a world that likes quick results and statistics-heavy newsletters with jaw-dropping stories. Our strategy has simply been to approach ministry among the poor as a long-term missionary endeavor. So we encourage our workers to raise financial support in order to create sustainability.

Set Realistic Goals—and Expectations

I remember sitting in a meeting in New York and hearing a church planter say that if we aren't seeing 200 people in our plant by the third year, then maybe we ought to question our call. Another planter told us he was "moving in faith" to a new area with a core team of 150 people.

Some American church planters once visited our service in Niddrie, where we had about 75 people in attendance. Afterward during lunch, one said he thought we'd be more successful if we had better musicians and brightened the place up a bit. I informed him that in housing-scheme terms, we are a megachurch!

When I hear stories of churches attracting hundreds to their launch services, I assume most of the people in attendance are Christians who have been part of other churches in the area. A church in a poor community is far less likely to have a large reservoir of Christians to draw from. It is likely to grow more slowly because it will have to grow through conversions. Certainly, God could send revival and shower us with thousands of converts. But barring something extraordinary, I will be delighted if we see pockets of 20 to 40 believers in multiple schemes after 10 years of work. That would constitute great success—even if it seems like a core group to some! Frankly, we put far too much pressure on church planters and revitalizers with unrealistic goals and expectations.

And when our expectations are unrealistic, we risk doing more harm than good in our church-planting efforts.

56

WHY PLANT CHURCHES IN SMALL TOWNS?

Dayton Hartman

"What? Why?"

That was the first response I heard from someone learning of the Acts 29 Rural Collective, whose focus is churches planting rural churches. Like most other people, they assumed effective church-planting strategies should only (or at least primarily) focus on metropolitan areas.

Sure enough, this was the response I received when I told people I wanted to plant a church in a small town. Instead, I was encouraged to head to the city where there would be more to do, more opportunities, more people to reach. For all but a few I spoke with, small-town ministry was not just an afterthought; it was never a thought.

Few ministries prioritize church-planting efforts to easily forgotten places. The assumption is that those living outside large cities have already been reached with the gospel, and that small towns are idyllic locales free from the brokenness that ravages cities.

The needs of rural communities, however, mirror those of big cities. Both populations experience crushing poverty (16.6 percent in rural communities versus 17.2 percent in large cities), racism (vestiges of the KKK and redlining remained part of "small-town America" long after the Civil Rights Act), and the need for better community development.

While Acts 29 helps churches plant churches in cities, they also understand the spiritual plight of small towns, forgotten places, rural communities, and secluded villages. Should we plant churches in major cities? Yes, but not at the expense of small communities, since small towns and rural communities are under-gospeled.

Plight of Small Towns

It's a radical misunderstanding of rural America's missiological landscape to assume that cities are in need and small towns are not. Ample opportunities exist for tangible ministry coupled with gospel proclamation. But we aren't planting enough gospel-centered churches to preach the gospel and meet needs as a physical manifestation of the Holy Spirit's renewing work.

Every year I've served in small towns of North Carolina, I've learned of a church in my denomination (Southern Baptist) closing. And when I look outside of my own tradition to other denominations, the numbers jump exponentially. The rate of decline is devastating. In South Carolina, my denomination witnessed a 130,000-person decline in church membership from 2012 to 2017.

The North American Mission Board issued a SEND Institute report which demonstrates that small towns and rural areas are far from being reached with the gospel.[45] A recent study conducted by Pew Research shows that even though rural America's population is growing, their counties are some of the least churched places in the United States.[46] Small towns are seeing churches close and divide when they need to be witnessing churches planted and multiplying.

Biblical Ethic for Small-Town Ministry

The Bible itself provides examples of aiming our efforts at rural communities. First, Jesus was from Nazareth. What

---

[45] Ed Stetzer, "Reaching and Revitalizing Rural America: Overcoming the Misconceptions of Idyllic Life and Gospel Saturation," *SEND Institute*, June 19, 2018: https://www.sendinstitute.org/revitalizing-rural-america-overcoming-the-misconceptions-of-idyllic-life-gospel-saturation/ accessed on Jan. 18, 2021.

[46] Bob Smietana, "America's Hidden Mission Field: Why We Need Rural Churches," *Christianity Today*, October 27, 2018: https://www.christianitytoday.com/edstetzer/2018/october/americas-hidden-mission-field-why-we-need-rural-churches.html accessed on Jan. 18, 2021.

do we know about it? Not much, except that it was full of goats (along with other livestock) and likely marked by crushing poverty. It was a forgettable place where few wanted to live. Which is why Nathanael famously asked, "What good can come from Nazareth?" (John 1:43–46).

Yet, the sovereign God of heaven chose an easily forgotten place for the Messiah to be raised. Like Nathanael, we wrongly limit the power of God to the places we prioritize. And if we're honest, those typically are the places we want to live, work, and play.

Second, much of Jesus's ministry occurred in small towns. Reading through the Gospel accounts, we see that Jesus wasn't spending his life in the major city centers (although he did minister in Jerusalem). Instead, his regular rhythm was engaging people in poor villages and small communities. The Scriptures are clear: Jesus loves unlovable and easily forgotten places because the gospel is good news for unlovable and easily forgotten people.

Need for Small-Town Church Planting

I know the cry of sociologists, anthropologists, and missiologists is "Go to the city. The world is rapidly urbanizing. The future is the city." To which I would reply: ever since the birth of the Roman Empire, people have predicted the demise of the village, the end of rural living, the annexing of small communities.

Nearly two millennia since the end of the Roman Empire, urbanization has continued, but small towns remain. And the people in small towns need the gospel just as desperately as city folk do.

Yes, let's take the good news that Jesus saves sinners to the epicenters of modern-day culture. But let's not forsake our neighbors in rural communities. Jesus prioritized bringing gospel grace to people in small towns—and we should, too.

57

DON'T GUT OR TRUNCATE THE GOSPEL

Bill Riedel

After months of pandemic challenges and a complete disruption in the pace of life, recent weeks have also brought an eruption of greater exposure to racial injustice, leading to protests worldwide. Racial injustice is not a new issue. What we see today is a new outcry over destruction that's been cultivated over centuries. Lord willing, it will lead to real change.

As a white pastor who planted a church in the heart of D.C., a city affectionately known as Chocolate City, I've had a lot to learn. Some of my own naivete and blind spots have been exposed, and surely more will be with time. As I've been learning, I've also been working to lead our church to a greater understanding of the fullness of the gospel as we live as sojourners and exiles in our cities (1 Pet. 2:9–11).

Too often, the people in our churches have been discipled more by political perspectives and platforms than by Scripture concerning justice in public life. Pastors have a responsibility to undercut partisan rhetoric and apply God's Word to real life. Church planters are uniquely positioned to shape the culture of new churches and to assert a biblically firm foundation capable of addressing whatever is happening culturally.

One familiar grid to understand the gospel's narrative (the story that runs throughout all Scripture) is: Creation, Fall, Redemption, and Restoration.

Christians who lean right and left have both deemphasized points of this complete narrative in harmful ways.

Temptation Toward a Gutted Gospel

Focusing only on *creation* and *restoration* results in a social gospel. The temptation is to overemphasize human ability to bring the eternal kingdom to bear today. While minimizing the atoning work of Jesus on the cross, the social gospel says we can and must restore all creation and administer all justice in this life. Leaders avoid preaching on God's holiness or human sin for fear of being offensive. They teach how to become better citizens without centering our need for a Savior.

This is the temptation of the Christian left. Follow it, and you might make disciples, but not of Jesus. The irony is that this focus looks to politics as savior. The perspective fails to account fully for human depravity and the need for a personal encounter with the Son of God. So it works to implement Christian perspectives without a call to Christ.

Temptation Toward a Truncated Gospel

On the other hand, some focus only on *fall* and *redemption*. The cry from the pulpit is, "You're a sinner! Repent!" Unfortunately, it often ends there. Christians in this perspective miss the beauty and significance of creation, and the hope of God's restorative work (Rom. 8:18–25). They minimize the call on God's people to correct oppression, seek justice, and protect the weak (Isa. 1:17). They also miss God's image and likeness in other people—an image that needs to be redeemed and restored, yet also reflects his beauty and glory.

The irony here is that over-conflation of civil religion into politics has wrongly divided biblical Christianity from speaking into politics at all. Calls to "Just preach the gospel!" are often more concerned with personal rights than the collective good, ignoring that the gospel is bigger than our individual salvation stories. This is the temptation of the Christian right. It's a truncated gospel that fails to connect Christ's work on the cross to his work through his people. Cries of "Just preach the gospel!" in the face of racial injustice too often represent a failure to love our neighbor. We're still stuck asking Jesus, "And who is my neighbor?" (Luke 10:29).

Power of the Gospel

To combat racial injustice, church planters must proclaim the whole gospel, showing the people in our churches and in our cities that the gospel speaks to our need now. All things are made by God to reflect his glory, and all people bear his image and likeness and are worthy of dignity and love. All creation has been affected by the power and dominion of sin. Total depravity means that every person, *and* the structures and systems of this world, are bent by sin.

Jesus endured the cross for us, where he was unjustly arrested, beaten, and killed by human authorities, even though he is the authority who sustained the life of his torturers. But death could not hold him down. Suffering, injustice, the powers of this world, and the Devil himself did not win, because Christ triumphed over them and now rules and reigns over all things. The kingship and anticipated return of Jesus frees us from fitting categorically into this world's systems and adapting the gospel to be palatable to either the right or the left, because our true and lasting citizenship is of a different kingdom.

Yes: listen, lament, and learn. Educate yourself where you may have ignorance or blind spots.[47] And then lead your church plant to actively work for the good of your city (Jer. 29:7–11), preaching the whole counsel of God. As we lead people to know and live in light of the fullness of the gospel—not pandering to cries to gut or truncate it—we'll find our prophetic voice and work for justice and healing as we anticipate the restoration of all things.

---

[47] For more, see Acts 29's "Recommended Resources on Race and Justice, *Acts 29*: https://www.acts29.com/resources-race-and-justice/ accessed on Jan. 18, 2021.

58

WE WILL NOT RAGE

J. A. Medders

The nations rage, the kingdoms totter; he utters his voice, the earth melts. The LORD of hosts is with us; the God of Jacob is our fortress.

– Psalm 46:6–7

Election Day in the United States is here. The news is spinning, minds are racing, affections are misfiring. While some of our neighbors are rejoicing, others are raging. All of us are probably exhausted from the adrenal-pumped arguments we see to the right and the left.

Where can we go in this political turmoil for a moment of refuge?

Right now, we can experience a renewing deep in our souls. Upheaval is not a time to wring our hands or throw them in the air. Upheaval can be a time of renewal. The key is to zoom out and catch a glimpse of a greater discombobulation than American politics.

Get Apocalyptic

In Psalm 46, the Sons of Korah invite us to sing along with a kind of unrest, chaos, and trouble that make our country's current moment resemble a stubbed big toe. Look at the situation the Sons of Korah are painting—the whole earth is on the fritz. ". . . though the earth gives way, though the mountains be moved into the heart of the sea, though its waters roar and foam, though the mountains tremble at its swelling" (vv. 2–3).

Pretend the earth's magnetic poles go haywire and the moon stops pulling the waves back into the ocean. Imagine Mount Kilimanjaro somehow sliding into the Indian Ocean. Picture the Grand Canyon collapsing in on itself, becoming a flat, dusty plain. Beauty and awe are now ashes and suds. Can it get any worse than the earth shutting down? Psalm 46 is apocalyptic; it's just what we need.

And yet, what tune are the Sons of Korah teaching us in Psalm 46? "God is our refuge and strength, a very present help in trouble. Therefore we will not fear though the earth gives way . . ." (vv. 1–2). Even if the earth loses its bearings, we will not fear. Our current cultural climate, while significant, is small potatoes compared to the meltdown of our planet in Psalm 46.

In light of this week, let's get more apocalyptic. If we allow ourselves to zoom out, lift up our eyes and assess reality, the people of God will see we have a reason to resist the rage of the nation, but to rejoice with heaven.

Get Still

It makes sense that "the nations rage and the kingdoms totter" (v. 6) since they have no bearing outside of themselves. When the dominos of life don't click and fall the way we want, it's disorienting. We all have neighbors raging—are we? The triune God is our real-time "present help" (v. 1) to keep us from joining the rage machine.

This is when the famous line of this Psalm kicks into gear: "Be still and know that I am God" (v. 10). We need this word. We especially need it today. Some take this verse as encouragement to get a cup of Ethiopian coffee and sit in the shade of a mossy oak tree. I'm all for it. However, nestled into the language of this Psalm is something more intense. It's a refusal to participate in the calamity, insanity, and bustle around us.

The Tanakh (Hebrew Bible) translates Psalm 46:10 this way: "Desist! Realize that I am God! I dominate the nations; I dominate the earth." Eugene Peterson put it this way: "Step out of the traffic! Take a long, loving look at me, your High God, above politics, above everything."

Psalm 46 is about more than simple stillness; it's a

stillness from messiness. It's resigning from the rage machine. It's stepping out of the madness, the media, the overcharged rhetoric, and taking a long and loving look at our God and rightly seeing reality. I'm not asking you to eject from culture. I'm inviting you to inject spiritual reality.

The Sons of Korah remind us of four truths to help us experience deep spiritual renewal amid any turbulence.

1. **God is our refuge (v. 1).** American politics cannot bring a sigh of relief and security to our souls. Only God renews us.
2. **God is our strength (v. 1).** Any other source of strength is a mistake. Partisan politics is a placebo, a sugar pill, for our sanity. God is how our hearts and souls thrive in these times.
3. **Our future is indestructible (v. 5).** God has fortified your future in his everlasting kingdom. Nothing can threaten the place Jesus has gone to prepare for you.
4. **The Lord of hosts is with us (v. 7).** No president or policy can match or evict the joy, sweetness, and comfort the commander of the cosmos, the risen Christ, gives his people.

Don't let temporal tides override the truth embedded in your heart. Refuse to ride the rage bus. Desist. Get out of the traffic. Get still and remember God. Renewal is there with him. As the old hymn teaches, "When all around my soul gives way, he then is all my hope and stay."

59

PASTORAL APOLOGETICS FOR A NEW ERA

Jonathan Dodson

The apologetics training I received in seminary is inadequate for my present ministry. This is no fault of my seminary; it's a reflection of how rapidly our society has changed over the past two decades.

In his survey of U.S. history from 2000 to the present, historian Philip Jenkins traces some seismic changes in technology, government, morality, and religion. He concludes: "The scale and speed of the accumulated power of transformation since 2000 really has no precedent." Jenkins further notes that it will take years to assess the full effect of this rapid change.[48]

This means everyone, including pastors and church planters, must catch up to these revolutions. One way to address cultural changes is to *listen* to people in our churches. When I moved to Austin, Texas, 15 years ago, I made a habit of asking people questions about their beliefs. In turn, they often asked about mine: Is the Bible reliable? Why is Christianity so narrow? Did Jesus really rise from the dead? Essentially, they were asking, is Christianity *true*?

Today, people are asking different questions. Considering the prospect of celibacy, my friend with same-sex attraction asks, "Does God want me to be lonely and unloved?" A frustrated person of color proclaims, "Preaching

---

[48] Philip Jenkins, *Rethinking a Nation: The United States in the 21st Century* (Red Globe Press, 2019), 3.

the gospel isn't enough. We need justice!" A woman in my city group inquires, "Why does it seem like the church is against women?" People want to know if Christianity is *good.*

Pastoring Toward the Good

We can respond to these questions with wisdom-packed one-liners, but that might hurt more than help. People need more than apologetic zingers and book recommendations. They're wondering if the new life that Christianity promises is a good life.

I needed to hear my gay friend's question, not only to answer him but also to identify, in a small way, with his feared prospect of a life of celibacy. I also needed to absorb how a person of color feels, not simply parse the differences between critical race theory and biblical truth. I need to know what it's like to ponder whether God prizes men more than women. Pastors, we need to sit with these questions—these people—to appreciate the depth and emotional complexity of our vocation.

As we pastor through the swift societal changes in sexuality, gender, racial identity, and politics, we're confronted with competing notions of good. For some, racial justice is the highest good. For others, it's political revolution. For still more, sexual and gender self-expression. These visions of goodness compete with Jesus's vision of goodness. We're called to shepherd others into his stunning vision of goodness while demonstrating the centrality of the gospel to the good life.

Recovering the Good

Where do these alternate ideas come from? We're oppressed by what sociologist Christopher Lasch describes as "transcendental attention to the self."[49] This attentiveness has a beat that, in the words of Tom Wolfe, "goes . . . Me . . . Me . . . Me . . . Me."[50] This me-fixation is apparent

---

[49] Christopher Lasch, *The Culture of Narcissism: American Life in an Age of Diminishing Expectations* (Norton, 2018), 14.

[50] Tom Wolfe, "The 'Me' Decade and the Third Great Awakening," *New York Magazine*, August 23, 1976: https://nymag.com/news/features/ 45938/

in how people tend to use the Bible today. Instead of looking to Scripture to shape our views, we often shape Scripture to suit our views. This leads us away from the authority and goodness of Christ.

While we may have a piece of what is good—justice, equality, freedom—under the authority of self, we wield it in unhelpful and harmful ways. We think our good must become *the* good. Our truth must become *the* truth. This oppresses others who don't share our truth, producing a religion that is acrimonious, divisive, self-righteous, and exhausting.

This, of course, is why Jesus died—to rescue us from transcendental self-interest and to rivet our attention on him. When we direct the attention meant for him to ourselves, we spoil his image. When we behold Jesus, though, he renews his image in us and we act more like him (Col. 3:10).

Speaking the Good

Jesus's response to evil wasn't just to use his "hands and feet." He also used his mouth: "And Jesus went throughout all the cities and villages, teaching in their synagogues and proclaiming the gospel of the kingdom and healing every disease and every affliction" (Matt. 9:35). Some mocked. Others marveled.

But Jesus *spoke*. His gospel challenged the prevailing notions of good. And so must we.

After spending considerable time with my gay friend, I explained to him that God doesn't want him to be lonely or unloved. Just the opposite! Jesus gave his life for sinners like my friend and me so that we could experience limitless love and ceaseless fellowship with the Holy Spirit.

Like Jesus, we must get close to people. Hiding behind the pulpit or always escaping to the study creates unhealthy distance between the sheep (including lost sheep) and the shepherd. Many are curious about truth and goodness. Let's position ourselves to be the ones speaking

---

accessed on Jan. 18, 2021.

into their struggles and answering their questions with biblical clarity and compassion.

Church planter, as you develop your apologetics to address the rapidly changing moral landscape, remember to embody what is true and good. Remember who is wholly and completely good. And help others find the answers to their questions in Scripture. After all, Christianity is good because it is true, and its truth is Christ.

60

STARTING CHURCHES IN A "FOLLOW YOUR HEART" AGE

Matt Hodges

Not long ago, relativism defined the cultural conversation. Truth was "unknowable." Perhaps it was somewhere "out there," but anyone's guess as to *where* was as good as the next.

This is no longer the case.

Today, we're in a new cultural moment—one marked not by relativism, but by a new phenomenon known as expressive individualism.[51] While relativism may label an assertion of external and objective truth as arrogant, expressive individualism calls it oppressive. The relativist asks, "Who's to say what's true?" The expressive individualist replies, "Me."

Look across the landscape of cultural artifacts, and you'll find the same motif time and again: Power and freedom are found in self-discovery. As Tim Keller notes, "The only heroic narrative we've got left in our culture is the individual looking inside, seeing who they want to be, and asserting that over and against everyone else in society."[52]

So we really have moved on from relativism: Truth is

---

[51] For more, see "Trevin Wax, Expressive Individualism: What Is It?", *The Gospel Coalition,* October 16, 2018: https://www.thegospelcoalition.org/blogs/trevin-wax/expressive-individualism-what-is-it/ accessed on Jan. 18, 2021.

[52] Tim Keller, Russell Moore, and Collin Hansen, "Following Jesus in an Age of Authenticity": https://www.youtube.com/watch?v=R_IBHXVfVeA accessed on Jan. 18, 2021.

now not only knowable, it's been found. All you have to do is look inside yourself.

Individualism and the Church

Many in the church can sniff out—even refute—relativism. We've been handed enough apologetic tools and basic reasoning skills to dismantle the notion that truth is subjective. Expressive individualism, however, is more insidious. It allows us to appear as if we're worshiping God, when in reality we're bowing to the god of self. It acknowledges the power of Jesus, but convinces us that he intends to use his power to further our own self-centered goals and aspirations. It agrees we can be certain about truth, but points to our own hearts as the source.

It's sobering to think about the church's collusion with this framework. Rather than pushing back against individualism, congregations often subtly encourage it. When we center everything, from Sundays to small groups, on the individual experience, we stoke the fire of self-worship. If we're not careful, we can betray the message that "Christ is king" with a method that says, "Actually, you are."

Deny Yourself

Biblically speaking, it's difficult to find two terms more antithetical than *self* and *church*. And it's not as though we must wade through cloaked language to discover this antithesis. When Jesus calls us into his church, his charge is not that we discover but deny ourselves (Matt. 16:24–25). Further, when Jesus enumerates the things that spring from our hearts, truth doesn't make the list. Only false testimony and evil thoughts do.

Or pull on any thread in Paul's epistles, and you'll find it connected to a call to pursue humble unity and consider others more significant than yourself. Simply put, a biblical understanding of what it means to believe in Jesus and belong to his church is incompatible with expressive individualism.

Truth is neither relative nor self-generated; it is knowable. In fact, it's touchable. Ultimate truth exists in the form of a man, the God-man—the one who died *for* our sinful hearts so that we could die *to* them.

The fruit-desiring, lie-believing, wilderness-wandering self is the very thing we bury as we are buried with Christ. His death for us becomes our death to self, and his new life becomes our new life—a life in which we deny ourselves instead of listening to ourselves, in which we take up our cross instead of taking up our dreams, and in which we follow him instead of following our hearts.

Church Planting's Counter-Culture

Church planting has always been central to Jesus's mission. But it's particularly helpful and corrective in today's cultural climate. As embodied creatures, we are formed by what we do. Our rhythms of life shape us from the outside in. What we do with our time, our hands, our lips, our money—all of it shapes our hearts. Just like the liturgy of a worship gathering, the method becomes part of the message. And both the method and also the message of church planting regularly remind us that we are not the point.

Planting a church requires a radical commitment to a unified, corporate identity. This commitment naturally undermines expressive individualism, since it simply won't allow us to place ourselves—our beliefs, our preferences, our desires—at the center of the church's reason for existence.

When we plant churches and press into the challenges, we invite our brothers and sisters into rhythms of life and ministry that will, slowly but surely, force the primacy of self to erode. And that will, time and again, yield the blessed—albeit painful—reminder that we are not, in fact, the arbiters of truth and goodness.

In a church plant, you have to strip away the superfluous for the sake of the essential. While there's nothing necessarily wrong with programs and production, the simplicity of a church plant offers a repeated invitation to forsake self-centeredness for self-denial.

Musical preferences begin to pale in comparison to the beautiful sound of a school cafeteria filling with gospel-proclaiming voices. Preaching "style" matters little when a living room is filled with those listening to their pastor faithfully mine the depths of God's Word week in and week out. Life as a part of a church plant has a way of forcing us to not only keep the truth of the gospel central, but also primary. And it teaches us, in both message *and* method, that we must daily trust our faithful King rather than our fickle selves.

At a time when the church is, lamentably, one of the first places to capitulate to individualism, church planting gives Christ's followers a chance to regularly exercise the much-needed practice of leading our hearts rather than following them. It takes whatever "truth" we think we've found within and subverts it with the pre-eminence of Christ and the truth of the gospel. And the more we keep that truth—*the* truth—at the forefront, the quicker the so-called truth we find "within" gets exposed for the counterfeit that it is.

TOPICAL INDEX

AUTHOR BIOGRAPHIES

Yancey Arrington is the teaching pastor at Clear Creek Community Church in Houston, Texas, where he has served since 1998. He's passionate about and coaches others on gospel centrality, preaching, theology, leadership, and church planting. Yancey is married to Jennefer, and has three sons. He's the author of *Preaching that Moves People* and *Tap: Defeating the Sins that Defeat You*. He also blogs at YanceyArrington.com. You can follow him on Twitter at @yanceyarrington.

Badi Badibanga is the executive ministry director at Bryanston Bible Church in Johannesburg, South Africa, and the founder and director of LiveAndLead.org. He is married to Stephanie, and they have three sons.

Kirsten Black and her husband, Vince, moved to Fort Collins, Colorado, in 2009 to plant The Town Church. Kirsten graduated with a master's degree in counseling from Covenant Theological Seminary in 2000 and currently serves as the director of Wives' Support for Acts 29. Kirsten and Vince are proud parents of their five boys.

Christy Britton is the content creator and editor for Acts 29. She's a member of Imago Dei Church in Raleigh, North Carolina, and serves as the discipleship classes coordinator. She's married to Stephen, and they're raising four boys together. You can follow her on Twitter at @christybritton6.

Landon Dennis is a church planter and pastor in the Middle East.

Jonathan Dodson (MDiv, ThM) is the founding pastor of City Life Church in Austin, Texas, and founder of Gospel-

Centered Discipleship. He's the author of several books, including *The Unbelievable Gospel*, *Here in Spirit*, and *Our Good Crisis: Overcoming Moral Chaos with the Beatitudes*.

David Doran Jr. serves as lead pastor of Resurrection Church in Lincoln Park, Michigan. He is married to Abigail, and they have four children. You can follow him on Twitter at @DavidinDetroit.

Dave Furman (ThM, Dallas Theological Seminary) serves as the senior pastor of Redeemer Church of Dubai in the United Arab Emirates. The church currently has more than 60 different nationalities gathering weekly from all around the world. In 2006 he developed a nerve disorder in his arms that renders both of them nearly disabled. He is the author of *Kiss the Wave: Embracing God in Your Trials* and *Being There: How to Love Those Who are Hurting*. He and his wife, Gloria, have been married for almost twenty years and have four children.

Jonathan (J. D.) Gilmore heads up Impatto (Acts 29 in Italy) and is the southeast Europe regional lead for Acts 29. Born to British missionary parents, J. D. grew up in Italy. He lives in Palermo, Italy, with his wife, Annette. He's planted LifeHope Church and is also involved with several developing initiatives of The Gospel Coalition in Europe.

Ben Hansen is the communications manager at 20schemes. He is married to Natalie and they have one son. He attends The Heights Church in St. Paul, MN.

Dayton Hartman is the lead pastor of Redeemer Church in Rocky Mount, North Carolina. He also serves as adjunct faculty for Southeastern Baptist Theological Seminary and Columbia International University. He is the author of *Lies Pastors Believe* and *Jesus Wins*. Dayton and his wife, Rebekah, have four sons. You can follow him on Twitter at @daytonhartman.

Noel Jesse Heikkinen is the teaching pastor at Riverview Church in the Lansing, Michigan area and serves as the US Midwest regional executive director for Acts 29. He is the author of two books (*Unchained* and *Wretched Saints*) and the host of the Recovering Hypocrite podcast. He and his wife, Grace, have four children.

Matt Hodges (MA, Dallas Theological Seminary) is the teaching pastor at Risen Church in northwest Houston. He is the author of *A Living Hope: Examining History's Most Important Event and What It Means for the World*. You can follow him on Twitter at @mahodges.

Reuben Hunter is the lead pastor of Trinity West Church in London. He is married to Louisa and has four children.

Bryan Laughlin is the lead pastor of Remnant Church in Richmond, Virginia, where he has served since planting the church in 2009. He's also the professor of Theology and Missiology at Grimké Seminary, Acts 29 co-director for Theological Training, and the network director of Acts 29 North Atlantic. Bryan and his wife, Paige, have four children.

Kyllum Lewis is the lead pastor of Life Centre Church in North Lakes, Brisbane, and also serves as the Queensland regional director for Acts 29 Australia, New Zealand, and Japan. Kyllum is married to Karly, and they have four children. He's passionate about portraying the beauty of the gospel and planting healthy churches. You can follow him on Facebook or at kyllumlewis.com.

Doug Logan, Jr. is an associate director for Acts 29 and has been in urban ministry for nearly 25 years. He serves as the president of Grimké Seminary in Richmond, Virginia, where he also serves as the dean of the Grimké School of Urban Ministry. He serves as the pastor for church planting at Remnant Church in Richmond, Virginia, and formerly served as senior pastor of Epiphany Camden in New Jersey, a church founded under his leadership in 2011. He is the author of *On the Block: Developing a Biblical Picture for Missional Engagement*. Doug and his wife, Angel, have been married since 1996 and have three adult sons and three grandchildren.

Mez McConnell is the senior pastor of Niddrie Community Church and director of 20schemes. He's also one of the directors of Church in Hard Places with Acts 29. Mez is the author of numerous books, including *The Creaking on the Stairs: Finding Faith in God Through Childhood Abuse* (Christian Focus), *Church in Hard Places* (Crossway), *Is There Anybody Out There?: A Journey from Despair to*

Hope (Christian Focus), *God: Is He Out There?* (Christian Focus/9Marks), and *War: Why Did Life Just Get Harder?* He's married to Miriam and they have two daughters and are also foster parents.

J. A. Medders serves on staff at Risen Church and the Risen Collective in Houston, TX. He's a PhD student in Biblical Spirituality at The Southern Baptist Theological Seminary. He is also the publishing manager and podcast producer for Acts 29 and hosts The Acts 29 Podcast. Jeff is the author of *Humble Calvinism* and *Gospel Formed.* You can follow his writing and monthly newsletter at spiritualtheology.net.

Tony Merida is the founding pastor of Imago Dei Church in Raleigh, North Carolina, director of Theological Training for Acts 29, dean of Grimké Seminary, and a Council member of The Gospel Coalition. He is the author of a number of books, including *The Christ-Centered Expositor, Ordinary,* and *Orphanology.* He and his wife, Kimberly, have five adopted children.

Raphael Mnkandhla serves as the lead pastor of City Church in Williamsport, Pennsylvania. He was born and raised in Bulawayo, Zimbabwe and is pursuing a PhD in Ministry at Midwestern Baptist Theological Seminary. Raphael is married to Heidi, and they have three sons, Judah, Cooper, Liam, and two daughters, Ellie and Aliyah.

Adam Muhtaseb (MDiv, Southeastern Baptist Theological Seminary) is the founding pastor of Redemption City Church in Baltimore, Maryland. He and his wife, Sherrie, have two sons, Aiden and Judah. You can follow him on Twitter at @Adam_Muhtaseb.

Jen Oshman has been a missionary and pastor's wife for over two decades on three continents. She's also a writer, speaker, and podcaster and especially passionate about encouraging women to deepen their faith and develop a biblical worldview. She is the author of *Enough About Me: Find Lasting Joy in the Age of Self* (Crossway, 2020) and *So Much More: Rejecting the Empty Promises of our Age and Embracing the Goodness of our God* (Crossway, 2022). Jen and her husband, Mark, currently reside with their daughters in Colorado where they planted Redemption Parker, an Acts 29 church.

Alyssa Poblete is the wife of Chris and mother of Geneva, Haddon, and Judson. Their family planted King's Cross Church in Orange County, California, in 2017. Alyssa studied English literature at Concordia University and worked in local church ministry for several years. Her passion is to see women connect the transforming power of the gospel to their everyday life though an ever-increasing understanding of God's Word. You can connect with her on Instagram at @alyssapoblete.

Doug Ponder (MDiv, ThM, Southeastern Seminary) is the teaching pastor at Remnant Church in Richmond, Virginia. He also serves as dean of faculty and professor of Biblical Studies at Grimké Seminary. He and his wife, Jessica, have four sons.

Adam Ramsey leads Liberti Church on the Gold Coast, Australia and also serves as the network director for Acts 29 Australia, New Zealand, and Japan. Adam really loves Jesus and is serious about joy. His favorite parts of life include being married to Kristina, making memories with their five kids, reading old books, exploring new places, preaching good news, equipping church planters, and laughing over a good meal.

Bill Riedel is the founding and lead pastor of Redemption Hill Church in Washington, D.C. He was formally trained at Trinity International University (BA) and Trinity Evangelical Divinity School (MDiv) and has served in ministry since 1998. He serves in Acts 29 as the D.C. area director and on the Acts 29 North Atlantic leadership team, as well as the board of the EFCA. You can follow him on Twitter at @BillRiedel.

Steve Robinson is the lead pastor of Cornerstone Church in Liverpool, England. He is also the director of the Cornerstone Collective. Steve is married to Sian, and they have four children. You can follow him on Twitter at @ste_robbo.

Tyler St. Clair is the lead pastor of Cornerstone Church Detroit in Detroit, Michigan. He also serves as the network lead for Church in Hard Places in Acts 29's U.S. Midwest region. Tyler is married to his best friend, Elita, and they have five amazing kids. You can follow him on Twitter at @tylerpsaint.

Dan Steel serves as the senior pastor of Magdalen Road Church in Oxford, England. Before returning to his hometown of Oxford, he helped plant Grace Church Dell Road in Birmingham, England. He and his wife, Zoe, have four children. You can follow him on Twitter at @dansteel77.

Amy Tyson is married to Adam and mom to Joel and Ethan. After living for nearly a decade in Sheffield, England, they now live in California where they're part of Sovereign Grace Church of Bakersfield. Amy previously taught English and is grateful for ten years of work in research, writing, and editing for Christian organizations.

Jan Vezikov is the lead pastor of Mosaic Boston (Brookline) in Boston, Massachusetts. He and his family moved to Boston to plant Mosaic in 2009. Jan was born in Estonia but grew up in Rhode Island. He is married to Tanya, and they have four daughters. You can follow him on Twitter at @JanVezikov.

Aaron Weiss is pastor of Mission Hill Church, which he planted in his hometown of Calgary, Alberta, in 2015. Aaron and his wife, Rachael, have two daughters.

Travis Whitehead is the director of operations for Acts 29 Emerging Regions, where he is honored to support church-planting efforts across much of Africa, Asia, and the Middle East. Travis is married to Janelle, and they have one daughter and a baby on the way. He has served as a church planter, bi-vocational pastor, and college minister in various locations, now as a Texan ex-pat in the Middle East.

Eddie Williams is the lead pastor of Bay City Church in San Francisco. Eddie is a former NFL player. He is married to Sarah, and they have three children. Eddie is a Bay Area native with a passion to better San Francisco, California.

ACKNOWLEDGMENTS

We must first say thank you to The Gospel Coalition. You gave our church-planting content a home for years and we enjoyed the partnership and greatly benefited from it. You helped us establish our online voice and reach a broader audience. A special thanks to Collin Hansen and Matt Smethurst, two brothers gifted in the editorial arts who helped make our content better. Without you, this book would not be possible.

Thank you to all the contributors in this book. Your stories and wisdom inspire many, and it's a joy to share your words in a book focusing on the continuing mission each of you has a passion for.

We're grateful to Bennett Hansen who served as Acts 29's original content editor. You served our ministry well and much of this content is the result of your hard work.

We owe a big thanks to Gospel-Centered Discipleship for publishing this book. You have been a joy to work with and helpful partners every step of the way. It's an honor to partner with you in this project.

Finally, thank you to Brian Howard, the Executive Director of Acts 29. Your leadership of Acts 29 has helped to move our global community forward, and your enthusiasm for this project sparked into life the idea of creating a book to highlight so many diverse voices from church leaders around the world.

ABOUT GOSPEL-CENTERED DISCIPLESHIP

You may have noticed that there are a lot of resources available for theological education, church planting, and missional church, but not for discipleship. We noticed too, so we started Gospel-Centered Discipleship to address the need for reliable resources on a whole range of discipleship issues.

When we use the term "gospel-centered," we aren't trying to divide Christians into camps, but to promote a way of following Jesus that is centered on the gospel of grace. While all disciples of Jesus believe the gospel is central to Christianity, we often live as if religious rules or spiritual license actually form the center of discipleship.

Jesus calls us to displace those things and replace them with the gospel. We're meant to apply the benefits of the gospel to our lives every day, not to merely bank on them for a single instance of "being saved." A gospel-centered disciple returns to the gospel over and over again, to receive, apply, and spread God's forgiveness and grace into every aspect of life.

GOSPEL-CENTERED DISCIPLESHIP RESOURCES

Visit GCDiscipleship.com/Books.

Many of us don't know our neighbors.

If we do know them, we aren't sure how to grow the relationship or talk about our faith with them. *Placed for a Purpose* provides a theologically rich framework for neighboring that helps people live missionally where God has placed them. Authors Chris and Elizabeth McKinney seek to provide a sustainable vision for the "low and slow" lifestyle of neighboring and supply practical tools that help people invest in their communities, value each step in the process, and build meaningful, gospel-motivated relationships with their fellow image-bearers right next door.

Identity is a hot topic these days, and many books have been written on it from a Christian perspective. However, virtually all of them begin in the present and move to the future. Almost none address the earliest chapters of your story where your identity took root. If much of the story you are writing is shaped by the story that was written for you, it makes sense to revisit your past in order to change unhelpful patterns of thought and behavior.

Tracing the Thread: Examining the Story of Self for Lasting Change will guide you back to the three chapters in your story which had the greatest bearing on identity formation—the love you received, the tribes you belonged to, and the voices you listened to—and help you uncover foundational errors in your identity beliefs.

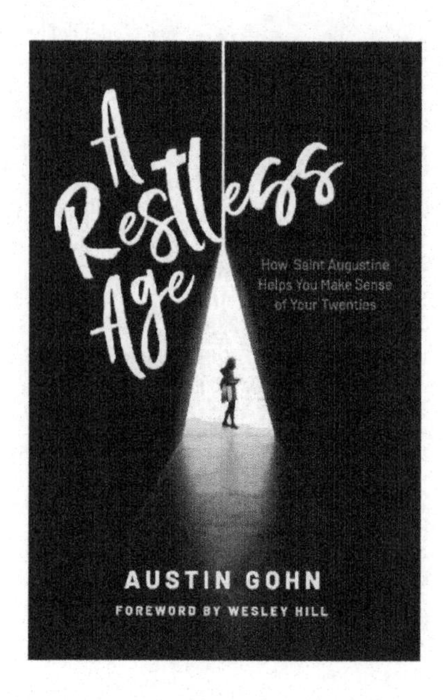

Do your twenties feel restless? You're not the first young adult to feel this way. Saint Augustine describes the same struggle in his Confessions, the most-read spiritual memoir in history. He experimented with different religious options, tried to break destructive habits, struggled to find the right friends, experienced a devastating breakup, and nearly burned out in his career—all before his thirty-second birthday. He spent his twenties looking for rest in all the wrong places.

In *A Restless Age*, Austin Gohn wades through Augustine's *Confessions* to show us how the five searches of young adulthood—answers, habits, belonging, love, and work—are actually searches for rest. "Our heart is restless," Augustine writes, "until it finds rest in you."

After fifteen plus years of vocational ministry, Ben Connelly had an epiphany. He had missed the great commission. He was really good at keeping Christians happy and really bad at making disciples. *A Pastor's Guide to Everyday Mission* helps those in paid ministry positions rediscover—and live—their life as God's missionaries, even as they minister to God's people.

Made in the USA
Monee, IL
06 April 2021